PRACTICE WISDOM

SAGE HUMAN SERVICES GUIDES, VOLUME 62

SAGE HUMAN SERVICES GUIDES

A series of books edited by ARMAND LAUFFER and CHARLES D. GARVIN. Published in cooperation with the University of Michigan School of Social Work and other organizations.

1: **GRANTSMANSHIP** *by Armand Lauffer* (second edition)
4: **SHARED DECISION MAKING** *by Frank F. Maple*
5: **VOLUNTEERS** *by Armand Lauffer and Sarah Gorodezky with Jay Callahan and Carla Overberger*
10: **GROUP PARTICIPATION** *by Harvey J. Bertcher*
11: **BE ASSERTIVE** *by Sandra Stone Sundel and Martin Sundel*
14: **NEEDS ASSESSMENT** *by Keith A. Neuber with William T. Atkins, James A. Jacobson, and Nicholas A. Reuterman*
15: **DEVELOPING CASEWORK SKILLS** *by James A. Pippin*
17: **EFFECTIVE MEETINGS** *by John E. Tropman*
19: **USING MICROCOMPUTERS IN SOCIAL AGENCIES** *by James B. Taylor*
20: **CHANGING ORGANIZATIONS AND COMMUNITY PROGRAMS** *by Jack Rothman, John L. Erlich, and Joseph G. Teresa*
24: **CHANGING THE SYSTEM** *by Milan J. Dluhy*
25: **HELPING WOMEN COPE WITH GRIEF** *by Phyllis R. Silverman*
27: **ORGANIZING FOR COMMUNITY ACTION** *by Steve Burghardt*
28: **AGENCIES WORKING TOGETHER** *by Robert J. Rossi, Kevin J. Gilmartin, and Charles W. Dayton*
29: **EVALUATING YOUR AGENCY'S PROGRAMS** *by Michael J. Austin, Gary Cox, Naomi Gottlieb, J. David Hawkins, Jean M. Kruzich, and Ronald Rauch*
30: **ASSESSMENT TOOLS** *by Armand Lauffer*
31: **UNDERSTANDING PROGRAM EVALUATION** *by Leonard Rutman and George Mowbray*
32: **UNDERSTANDING SOCIAL NETWORKS** *by Lambert Maguire*
33: **FAMILY ASSESSMENT** *by Adele M. Holman*
35: **SUPERVISION** *by Eileen Gambrill and Theodore J. Stein*
36: **BUILDING SUPPORT NETWORKS FOR THE ELDERLY** *by David E. Biegel, Barbara K. Shore, and Elizabeth Gordon*
37: **STRESS MANAGEMENT FOR HUMAN SERVICES** *by Richard E. Farmer, Lynn Hunt Monohan, and Reinhold W. Hekeler*
38: **FAMILY CAREGIVERS AND DEPENDENT ELDERLY** *by Dianne Springer and Timothy H. Brubaker*
39: **DESIGNING AND IMPLEMENTING PROCEDURES FOR HEALTH AND HUMAN SERVICES** *by Morris Schaefer*

40: **GROUP THERAPY WITH ALCOHOLICS** *by Baruch Levine and Virginia Gallogly*
41: **DYNAMIC INTERVIEWING** *by Frank F. Maple*
42: **THERAPEUTIC PRINCIPLES IN PRACTICE** *by Herbert S. Strean*
43: **CAREERS, COLLEAGUES, AND CONFLICTS** *by Armand Lauffer*
44: **PURCHASE OF SERVICE CONTRACTING** *by Peter M. Kettner and Lawrence L. Martin*
45: **TREATING ANXIETY DISORDERS** *by Bruce A. Thyer*
46: **TREATING ALCOHOLISM** *by Norman K. Denzin*
47: **WORKING UNDER THE SAFETY NET** *by Steve Burghardt and Michael Fabricant*
48: **MANAGING HUMAN SERVICES PERSONNEL** *by Peter J. Pecora and Michael J. Austin*
49: **IMPLEMENTING CHANGE IN SERVICE PROGRAMS** *by Morris Schaefer*
50: **PLANNING FOR RESEARCH** *by Raymond M. Berger and Michael A. Patchner*
51: **IMPLEMENTING THE RESEARCH PLAN** *by Raymond M. Berger and Michael A. Patchner*
52: **MANAGING CONFLICT** *by Herb Bisno*
53: **STRATEGIES FOR HELPING VICTIMS OF ELDER MISTREATMENT** *by Risa S. Breckman and Ronald D. Adelman*
54: **COMPUTERIZING YOUR AGENCY'S INFORMATION SYSTEM** *by Denise E. Bronson, Donald C. Pelz, and Eileen Trzcinski*
55: **HOW PERSONAL GROWTH AND TASK GROUPS WORK** *by Robert K. Conyne*
56: **COMMUNICATION BASICS FOR HUMAN SERVICE PROFESSIONALS** *by Elam Nunnally and Caryl Moy*
57: **COMMUNICATION DISORDERS IN AGING** *edited by Raymond H. Hull and Kathleen M. Griffin*
58: **THE PRACTICE OF CASE MANAGEMENT** *by David P. Moxley*
59: **MEASUREMENT IN DIRECT PRACTICE** *by Betty J. Blythe and Tony Tripodi*
60: **BUILDING COALITIONS IN THE HUMAN SERVICES** *by Milan J. Dluhy with the assistance of Sanford L. Kravitz*
61: **PSYCHIATRIC MEDICATIONS** *by Kenneth J. Bender*
62: **PRACTICE WISDOM** *by Donald F. Krill*

A **SAGE** HUMAN SERVICES GUIDE **62**

PRACTICE WISDOM

A Guide for Helping Professionals

Donald F. KRILL

Published in cooperation with the University of Michigan School of Social Work

SAGE PUBLICATIONS
The International Professional Publishers
Newbury Park   London   New Delhi

For information address:

SAGE Publications, Inc.
2111 West Hillcrest Drive
Newbury Park, California 91320

SAGE Publications Ltd.
28 Banner Street
London EC1Y 8QE
England

SAGE Publications India Pvt. Ltd.
M-32 Market
Greater Kailash I
New Delhi 110 048 India

Printed in the United States of America

Library of Congress Cataloging-in-Publication Data

Krill, Donald F.
    Practice wisdom: a guide for helping professionals / Donald F. Krill.
        p. cm. — (Sage human services guides; v. 62)
        Includes bibliographical references (p.   ) and index.
        "Published in cooperation with the University of Michigan School
            of Social Work."
        ISBN 0-8039-3606-0
        1. Social service — Psychological aspects. 2. Human services —
    Psychological aspects. I. University of Michigan. School of
    Social Work. II. Title. III. Series
    HV40.K72 1990
    361.3 — dc20   90-8606
                                                                    CIP

FIRST PRINTING, 1990

Sage Production Editor: Astrid Virding

CONTENTS

Preface   9

Introduction   11

1. Who Are You?   17
   Looking into Yourself   21

2. Survival and Creativity   26
   Journal Responses to Exercises   26
   Discussion   29

3. Personal Freedom   33
   Journal Responses to Exercises   33

4. The Person Is Not the Category   40
   Journal Responses to Exercises   42
   Problem Exploration Exercises   43
   Journal Responses   48
   New Exercise   49

5. Guilt and Its Resolution   50
   Journal Responses to Exercise   53

6. Facilitating Change   56
   Theoretical Issues Regarding Change   57
   Inner Chatter and Beyond   65

7. Professional Intensity   68
   Professional Intensity and Use of Self   71
   Assignments   75

8. Matters of Spirituality   77

9   Becoming a Sojourner 80
    Questions for Your Personal Path 85
10 Application to Teaching of Languages 88
    Employee Assistance Programs 91
    Adjustment and Proactive Defense of Change 93
    Workforce 2 000 95
    Summary 97
11 Conclusion 99

PREFACE

This book is the outgrowth of 15 years of experimentation with the development and teaching of a course titled Existential Social Work. While this course has been taught in a graduate program for social work students, it is relevant for students of any "professional helper" training as well as for professionals seeking new dimensions for their own staff development. Chapters 10 through 13 apply the material for use with the lay public, by focusing upon issues of burnout and addiction as often encountered in employee assistance training programs.

The reference list provides sources for the main ideas posed in the book. The exercises have been derived from a number of sources. When they are utilized here in the manner I originally learned them, the sources are cited. For the most part, however, the exercises have been modified and redesigned for the purpose of training helping professionals in self-awareness while at the same time integrating exercise results with the tools of helping professions: theory, professional use of self, and the application of helping techniques.

I do wish to acknowledge with gratitude some training experiences that have undoubtedly affected the development of many of the exercises in this volume. I greatly value my exposure to meditation training with Alan Watts, Phillip Kapleau, Thomas Keating, Theophane the Monk, the Forum Experience, Gestalt, and psychodrama training with Jim Thursby and Carl Hollander. The most important training experience, however, has been work with students in this course, reading their journals and sharing in their discussions of exercise results.

Excerpts from student journals are included here to provide the reader with comparative responses to exercises. A reader may learn from this book, doing the exercises alone or with another person, and have the benefit of knowing how other students describe their work with

But suppose the most successful, most spontaneous and alive form of helping depends upon the integration of theory, religion/philosophy, and subjective experience? Suppose this integration is the basis of charisma (power of influence), of creativity (helping as an art), and of self-esteem (personal power)? If this is so, we would have to say that training programs are sadly lacking, as they address only one of these three knowledge areas with any depth and consistency.

There is strong evidence, based in research, that supports this very deficit in professional education. Well known for over a decade now is the researched opinion concerning the effectiveness of psychotherapy and social casework: In study after study it has been shown that no particular theory or therapy model proves itself more or less effective than any other (Krill, 1986, chap. 3). The obvious conclusion from this is that theory is not the key ingredient to effective practice. It is far more likely that the crucial factor is something highly personal—how a particular worker integrates what he or she knows about him- or herself and the client, and the present happening between the two (the creative factor). This has often been referred to as "practice wisdom."

There is little doubt that practice wisdom develops over time. It results from a worker's being open to continued learning from each new client situation as well as to his or her own personal changing subjective experience. It includes an ongoing effort at learning and integrating from the three knowledge areas about human experience. Both theory and philosophy or religious understanding can often help us manage the frustrating confusions of our subjective experience.

Practice wisdom, however, does not simply emerge naturally. Why do some attain it and others not? Why are so many practicing professionals burned out, narrowly rigid and judgmental, or frantically searching for that ever-elusive key to effective practice? The closest many professionals come to looking at the knowledge areas of religion/philosophy and subjective experience is in their personal psychotherapy. But even then the knowledge is focused upon their own problems rather than upon a more creative use of themselves in their professional practices.

THE SCOPE OF THE BOOK

I believe that both graduate students and professional helpers can be *taught* the ingredients of practice wisdom. They need not wait for a accumulation of years of experience. Practice wisdom can begin immediately, for it is a matter of knowing how to acquire and integrate knowledge in the three areas mentioned above. It is not a matter of *gaining* wisdom, but rather of entering upon a way of *growing* wisdom. I am not referring to any "new age" divine wisdom; this is something quite human and practical.

During the past 15 years I have taught a course titled Existential Social Work. The content of the class has meandered from discussion of philosophical/religious ideas to theory comparisons, to personal awareness exercises, to use of role plays, journals, and tapes, and an eclectic emphasis on utilizing a variety of known helping techniques.

In recent years I have focused the learning more and more upon the knowledge areas of subjective experience and religion/philosophy, while always helping students connect these to client understanding and use of self in practice situations. Students pick partners with whom they share the results of weekly personal awareness exercises. Every three or four weeks each student submits a journal to me that summarizes the results of these same weekly exercises. Students' journals also include their responses to course content, reading, and the shared experiences with their partners.

A further development of this style of learning has been my teaching of seminars on burnout and addiction to company employee programs and to staffs of professional helping agencies. In the introductory presentations of these seminars, both burnout and addiction are interpreted in the broadest possible way. Almost everyone can see themselves suffering, or having suffered, from one (if not both) of these maladies. Follow-up groups are organized for those who wish to pursue an experiential program not unlike many of the class exercises mentioned above. Issues of both burnout and addiction are related to personal belief systems, and these are examined in relation to overarching ideals held by group members. Work with professional staffs seeks to integrate the three knowledge areas of theory, religion/philosophy, and subjective experience with practice opportunities. The program for non-helping professionals maintains the focus on burnout and addiction without relating ideas to the professional helping process.

This book includes the ideas as well as exercises that are utilized in both the classroom for graduate students and the seminars for professional staffs and employee assistance programs. Excerpts from student journals illustrate how students experience the integrating process itself.

The major segment of the book will address the reader as a student who is interested in pursuing a path of self-knowledge by participating in suggested exercises and by reflecting upon ideas posed. The later segment of the book provides a model for training that can be used by students or professionals who are in work situations that include opportunities to train laypeople. The Appendix is provided specifically for faculty or helping professionals who wish to use content from this book for their own classes or staff development programs.

Chapter 1

WHO ARE YOU?

As a student, you may wish to use the content of this book for your personal search, as a complement to your course of studies, or as a workbook guide in relation to a specific course on self-awareness offered by your educational institution. In any case, you will find it extremely useful to have at least one other student pursue this study with you. Both of you will benefit from sharing your exercise experiences as well as from discussing many of the provocative ideas set forth. For those who elect to pursue their personal searches alone, I include samples of student reactions to exercises extracted from journals shared with me by students who took my course.

You will need to begin and maintain a personal journal of your exercise responses. Since the road to practice wisdom is an integrative effort, your journal will provide you a most useful tool for playing with ideas. As indicated in the Introduction, the idea areas of importance include theory, religious and/or philosophical perspectives, and your personal, subjective encounters with yourself. These last will occur in relation to your exercise efforts as well as in your practice with clients. If you are fortunate enough to find a student partner who shares in this practice wisdom search with you, you will quickly discover an added dimension of subjective encounter whenever the two of you share your exercise results.

What is meant by *subjective experience*?

> *Subjectivity*
>
> passion
> memory pool
> archetype images
> freedom of choice

Kirkegaard's famous declaration "Truth is subjectivity" (Reinhardt, 1960, pp. 23-58) was an appreciation of the uniqueness of each person's view of the world (this is the basic premise of phenomenology). For Kirkegaard, of course, it was not enough to appreciate one's personal worldview; one had to take responsibility for being the creator of it as well.

Consider the four forms of subjective experience indicated above and add to the list if you believe it to be too limiting. Here are some expanded definitions for your reflections.

Passion. This is a driving force within us, experienced also as desire, wants, needs, and demands. The object of passion may be many different things (e.g., sexual fulfillment, survival, power, relatedness, meaning, God, pleasure).

Memory pool. An individual's memory pool is made up of all that he or she already knows, the conclusions and meanings made from previous experiences. It is the basis for the individual's beliefs and related repetitive behavior patterns that seek specific valued experiences and avoidance of negative ones. Who we "think" we are, the roles we must take, and how we must deal with the world around us are all prescribed by this memory pool.

Archetype images. These are guiding cues or messages from the individual's subconscious, beyond his or her memory pool. They provide hints about one's potential (for both good and evil), resulting from some creative-integrative process occurring deep within the psyche. We encounter archetype images in dreams, fantasies, and our attraction to certain heroic types or myths and symbols that possess a special potency for us.

Freedom of choice. Despite the perplexities of freedom versus determination, we all experience moments of choice for which we are able to take responsibility. We may not agree with Sartre's paradoxical dictum, We are condemned to freedom whether we like it or not (Streller, 1960), but even behaviorists seem to accept the reality of choice, as evidenced in the wedding between behaviorists and cognitive theorists.

Now we move to the next rather basic question: What is meant by reality? Here is a philosophical and/or religious point of departure.

> *What Is Real?*
> known/unknown
> relative values/absolute values
> the absurd/destiny
> profane/sacred
> *tonal/nagual*
> left-brain thinking/right-brain thinking

You probably will not be familiar with the meanings of all of these pairs, but will know one or two of them. You may wish to add other pairs to the list. Reflect upon the way you usually perceive reality. There is not simply that ordinary, everyday experience that we all share, some objective reality common to everyone. There are special moments of intensity, ecstasy, beauty, rhythm, compassion, transcendence, connectedness, captivating truth, and horror that we often refer to as different from the ordinary. Maslow (1962) labeled many of these "peak experiences" as a way of speaking in secular terms of what are often described as spiritual, creative, or mystical experiences. Here, too, we have the philosopher's quest for truth.

Next, consider these pessimistic themes of some existential philosophers and authors. You may be familiar with these from undergraduate philosophy courses or from modern theater, art, and novels. They challenge some of the buoyant optimism common in conversations heard in schools of social work.

> *Existential Themes*
>
> | meaninglessness | |
> |---|---|
> | detachment | Albert Camus |
> | innocence | Joseph Heller |
> | absurdity | |
> | | |
> | confusion | Samuel Beckett |
> | despair | Franz Kafka |
> | guilt | Søren Kirkegaard |
> | powerlessness | |
> | | |
> | rebellion | Fyodor Dostoyevski |
> | outrageous behavior | Jean Genet |
> | | Norman Mailer |

These existential themes relate to a common concern. We live in a society that reinforces a set of values challenged by these writers. We imagine that we are a part of a society of continuing progress. Happiness can be achieved, controlled, and secured by means of technology, reason, and planned organizational and institutional arrangements. Social problems, war, and the gradual destruction of the environment are merely symptoms that we are not yet progressing correctly. What is needed is more education, more liberation, more social programs, more psychological help. The existentialists challenge these hopes, suggesting that the problem is the human condition itself. Both religious and nonreligious existentialists agree that we moderns are living out of a distorted view of reality. These views are poignantly described in the context of modern psychology (especially that of Freud and Rank) by Ernest Becker in his Pulitzer Prize-winning book, *The Denial of Death* (1973).

Another means of conveying this existential perspective that is more psychological, less philosophical, is found in the four layers of awareness enumerated by the Gestalt therapist Fredrick Perls (1969, chap. 4).

Layers of Awareness
social
phobic
implosive
explosive

Social awareness. This is the way we habitually experience ourselves and the world around us. This is characterized by repetitive beliefs, gamelike manipulations, and self-deceptions. We portray a fixed "story" about ourselves based upon accumulated judgments, beliefs, conclusions. Here is our secure, everyday experiencing.

Phobic awareness. This is the anxiety layer, touched off by disconcerting experiences from both outside and within ourselves. Doubts surface as our prized "world design" is shaken. Our temptation is to run for cover, to hide out once more in our secured identity. We may use avoidance defenses, addictions, and manipulations of relationships and activities to accomplish this.

Implosive awareness. If, on the other hand, we choose (or are propelled into) the void that lies outside our usual identity sense, we experience the "death" or implosive layer. Here we find ourselves in despair, helpless to know our way out. Our usual identity conclusions appear now as masks, illusions, faulty values, empty gestures. We feel dread before a great mystery, humiliation in relation to our favored life-style. Yet somehow, in the very midst of this negativeness there is also a strange affirming openness toward life.

Explosive awareness. Letting go of our habitual pride, hopes, and fears, we begin to act out of new potentialities. We are responsively available to others and to our environment. A new honesty and an "I-thou" way of relating emerges. We feel connected in more creative and integrative ways with our own integrity as well as with our surroundings.

These layers of awareness need not be interpreted as some full-fledged conversion, or enlightenment, experience. While that is a rare possibility for some people, a reading of Perls's (1969) own autobiography certainly does not reveal an enlightened being. We usually refer to this change process as passing through some troubling disillusionment and, as a result of an intense inner struggle, arriving at a new point of expanded, potent insights.

LOOKING INTO YOURSELF

Now, let yourself consider two important aspects of your own experience. The first we will label *world design*, or security images. It is the repetitive sense of personal identity based on survival needs, and its aim is to secure and protect a predictable sense of who one is. The second we will, for the moment, not label, but refer to as that self that occurs in peak or transcendental experiences.

Here is your first exercise. It would be useful for you to take a break from your reading for a few hours or days and do the exercise before continuing the reading.

Inner chatter awareness. Attend to your own thinking and fantasy process periodically, especially when there is no particular need to be thinking about anything. Note what this use of thinking or fantasy seems to be doing for you. Categorize your most common experiences (criticizing, stroking, worrying, regretting, escaping, and so on).

The inner chatter awareness exercise brings to your awareness the activity of the mind—how it remains busy even at times when there is no special reason for thinking or fantasizing. Inner chatter may be thought of as the cement we all use to keep our security images patched together. We are often uncomfortable with inner voids, or silences, so we reassure ourselves as to the solidity and continuity of our identity.

Various theories describe world design in different terms. It is useful to consider some of these variations.

> *World Design: Protection and Survival*
>
> social self
> repetition-compulsion defense system
> life script
> fixed roles
> persona/shadow
> ego states (parent/adult/child)
> melodrama (story)
> irrational beliefs
> reinforced behavioral patterns
> bad faith (inauthentic living)
> character armor

World design stems from two major forces: our inner need for "hideouts" that reduce and help us manage our life experiences, and those social and societal reinforcements that invite, seduce, pressure, oppress, and sometimes physically force our conformity to defined values. Over time these two forces appear not in great opposition, but find a rather happy, if mindless, wedding together.

Ernest Becker's (1973) conception of "hideouts" emphasizes our need as finite human beings to control the extent and intensity of input from life situations that come our way. We are too easily overwhelmed by both the awesomeness and the horror of the universe. The fragility, unpredictability, contingency, and essential dependency of the human creature are too much. Death awaits, its time uncertain. Our identity images, roles beliefs, habit patterns, activities, desires, use of our body, memory-constructed conclusions are the warp and woof of our world design. We seek a secured, even solidified notion of who we are. This conceptualization defines how we should evaluate life happenings. It goes a step further, for even the way we use our awareness is largely controlled by our world design.

You may do this next exercise alone, or share it aloud with a companion who is willing to do the same exercise and share aloud with you. This exercise is utilized in Gestalt therapy training (Fagan & Shepard, 1970, chap. 21).

Now I am aware of . . . . In free-association style, do a series of sentences beginning with "Now I am aware of . . . " and end each sentence in whatever way you wish. Continue this process for three or four minutes. Do this exercise before reading further.

There is no correct way to do this exercise. Whatever points of awareness emerge for you are sufficient. Your experience, however, will be notably different from your partner's (if you have one) in certain respects. Your responses will probably even differ in some ways if you do this same exercise again tomorrow (especially so if your mood is different). Do you find that your foci are upon bodily sensations, outside stimuli, self-conscious thinking or feelings, fantasies?

World design is a normal development of the personality. It enables one to define an ideal and related roles so as to be able to survive and later function in the world. The failure to develop a clear sense of one's own identity, as seen at times among both psychotic and developmentally handicapped people, seriously limits one's ability to survive independently in society.

Social and societal value reinforcement is an immensely powerful process. It is also so subtly deceptive and manipulative that we are usually not even aware of its daily occurrences. We have little trouble resisting oppositional values that disturb us, from friends, family, our work or professional associates, support groups, professional helpers, and the entertainment/art/news media. But when our own identity conclusions are matched to a comforting fit with any of these social reinforcers, we are seldom aware of how we use (and are used by) these forces to limit our own awareness and potential growth. When we take a "retreat" for a weekend away from telephones, newspapers, television, friends, family, and job reminders, we become aware of just how powerful these forces have been upon our sense of self. We have a glimmer of the extent of exhaustion, dullness, rigidity, and alienation produced by the self-made prison of overused world design.

In contrast to this familiar sense of world design, or everyday identity, there are *peak experiences*. Reflect upon a moment in your life when you clearly stepped out of your ordinary way of experiencing yourself. The occurrence may have been positive or negative. Did it involve beauty in nature, rhythm in physical activity, intimacy with another person, creativity in the arts, a catastrophe of nature producing total helplessness, an accident, some personal conversion experience?

Now, let's do an exercise in which you will invite, and possibly experience, a state of mind similar to what occurs with a peak experience.

Meditative experience. Sit comfortably with head erect. Focus your attention on some object in the room by both looking at it and thinking about it. Analyze it in terms of color, size, texture, use, origin, odor, and so on.

Now recall someone you are acquainted with, but don't know well. Stereotype this person without regard to accuracy and compare him or her to yourself.

Close your eyes and attend to points of tension in your body. Also, note thoughts and feelings that are present for you. Imagine a large balloon that you can inflate with helium. As you inflate it, insert your thoughts, feelings, and tensions into it as well. Seal the balloon and let it float into the air.

Now attend to sounds. Let sound become your focus of attention. Notice thoughts, feelings, fantasies, and let them go by as you return your attention to sounds. Notice your breathing.

You may now use the here and now of sounds, breathing, or both as your focal point that allows you to let thoughts pass by without your following them. Stay with this experience for about five minutes.

When you open your eyes, look at the object in the room you observed and analyzed earlier. This time you may look at it without thinking about it.

Now recall your acquaintance's face again, this time without thinking about him or her.

––––––––

Did you notice differences in the various phases of the exercise? How did you perceive the object and your acquaintance differently at the end of the exercise in contrast to the early phase? Did your focus on sounds and/or breathing enable you to let go of some of your thoughts, feelings, and tensions? Thinking about an object, another person, or yourself tends to create judgments, which in turn arouse feelings or sensations of discomfort. To simply be with the here-and-now experience of that same object, person, or yourself reduces tension and often leaves you in a state of peace and acceptance.

Before you read the next chapter there are three more exercises for you to do and record in your journal. The first of these is an extension of the meditation exercise you just completed. The purpose of the exercise is to provide you with some immediate practical application to your work with others, professionally.

Being with a client without thinking. Be with a client without thinking about the client and without thinking about yourself. Do this for as long as you are comfortable with it, which may be only a matter of seconds or minutes. As you were with an object at the end of the meditative experience, now be with a client. Let the client be the focus of your attention rather than your thinking—analyzing, planning, and so on. If you have no client, do this in the midst of a conversation with a friend. Empathy is a process of letting go of one's own inner chatter in order to be with a client fully.

The next exercise for your journal will acquaint you with some key values of your personal world design. It may also acquaint you with some characteristics of archetype images that provide you with inspirational direction.

Heroes, heroines, models. Off the top of your head, list the important characters of your life, fictional or nonfictional, famous or not. Select examples from different age periods. Cross out those names you seem to no longer need (those you have outgrown). From the remaining names, describe the major characteristics of these people that seem important to you.

Do not skip this exercise because you think it too obvious or you do not wish to take the time. Allot yourself at least 15 minutes to do the exercise. You will be using the results of this exercise later in the book, although the experience of it right now is important for your expanding sense of world design, or security images.

The final exercise for this chapter provides you with another, more subtle and indirect, means of acquainting yourself with your personal world design.

Problematic inner chatter. Notice a time when you are painfully upset, either physically or emotionally. Attend to your thinking or fantasy. What are you saying to yourself? What value position or positions are revealed by this inner chatter? How do you want things, or yourself, to be?

Like it or not, chatter related to the experience of pain or frustration will reveal one or more value positions held dear to your heart. It is likely that such value positions may differ significantly from the characteristics of your world design noted in your response to the exercise on heroes, heroines, and models. You are beginning to appreciate the complexity of your world design patterns.

In the next chapter you will have an opportunity to compare your exercise responses to those of other students. You will also be building a clearer conception of how your world design operates. Doing these exercises carefully will have a natural carryover for your application to client understanding.

Chapter 2

SURVIVAL AND CREATIVITY

The first segment of work focused upon two common subjective experiences, the self-created yet habitually maintained world design, and the more elusive yet quite real sense of occasional self-transcendence. Now, in this second segment, you will begin to look more closely at your valuing process.

We will begin with journal feedback from other students on most of the exercises you have already accomplished. Of course, different students have varied reactions to each exercise. Do not worry about comparing your experiences with the experiences of others. These very differences are quite important for learning. Your own responses to the exercises are most important, because they reveal where you are in relation to the path toward practice wisdom. To grow, rather than resist, you need to begin with an acceptance and even an affirmation of your own personal starting point. The examples reviewed here are not necessarily typical. Differing responses have been selected for the purposes of your learning, not for your making comparisons. Excerpts from the journals of both male and female students of widely different ages are included.

JOURNAL RESPONSES TO EXERCISES

HEROES, HEROINES, AND MODELS

Was initially saddened to see so few women on the list; felt better when I saw the common denominators among my heroes/heroines: the categories seem to be those of devotion to the betterment of humankind, creative artists, and those who flaunted the conventions/thought of their time. The women on the list share the above qualities. The down side: most of them had limited relationships—or functioned outside that realm altogether. These women are, as well, by and large either physically, emotionally, or creatively courageous.

I admire people who are more accepting of life and what it brings to them, yet I have found that people who are easier on themselves are often unmotivated. I know there is a balance and I have yet to find it. The main qualities I have targeted for the people I admire are: responsibility for themselves and others; willingness to risk; self-motivation; acceptance of pain and suffering as a part of life; people who have ethics and morals, and live by them; people who have a somewhat free and easy attitude toward life; people who know how to play, and appreciate life; people with a strong faith and trust in God; and people who are disciplined.

INNER CHATTER AWARENESS

At work I catch myself thinking about my self-confidence and self-concept. Both are at this time rather weak and I wonder if these thoughts, and how these thoughts, may interfere with my work. I find that it is very difficult for me to forgive myself, whereas if I had seen someone else do the same, I would say "no problem" and be forgiving or understanding, or I am more tolerant of others than I am of myself. I strive for perfection constantly, knowing one can never meet it and still being upset with myself if I don't reach it. Then I say to myself that as long as I strive for perfection, I'll always be giving my task 100% effort and that what I end up with will be my best at that time.

I've always thought of inner chatter as being primarily negative because for myself I've thought it was something I needed to change. I repeatedly put myself down for always being late. I'm not beating myself up about it as much as I used to but this isn't enough, as I'd truly like to break this habit. A tape I frequently play is around being controlling, and this I do beat myself up about. I also have one about being insecure and lacking in self-confidence, primarily professionally. For years I've felt more experience and more education would cure this, but I'm beginning to think it goes deeper than that. I have been hesitant in sharing another image that would fit into the category of inner chatter. Frequently while driving I have this image of allowing myself to release control of my driving and crash, into a guard rail, into another car, or usually, off the road or over a cliff. My original thoughts about this were that I could lay in a hospital bed and receive lots of attention, and be relieved of my responsibilities. (As I'm typing this several weeks after originally writing it, I can see that it may be tied to my great need to have people accept me just for me and to not have that acceptance tied to what I'm doing, how good or successful

I am, how productive I am, how hard I'm working.) There's also some fear that these images are tied to some death wish, whatever that is.

My inner chatter seems to consist of comments to myself on what has happened, is happening, or is going to (may) happen. It consists of comments, songs (the words of which contain my comment), and, occasionally, images. I use this inner chatter to frame my world, to give it meaning. The meanings come from the "tapes" I've integrated from significant others and experiences through the years and are made up of expectations about the world, other people, and myself—how things "ought" to be. From this I know how to react. Without it, I feel disorientated and unprepared for dealing with my interactions with others.

PROBLEMATIC INNER CHATTER

Recently, I had an experience of terrific emotional pain, and at that moment my inner chatter was almost degrading. It gave me the old, old messages, in an instant, and told me that I really was not "good enough," and that life is just too hard. It was very positive for me to realize, though, that in addition to my negative "split-second" response, another side of me was saying, "You have a right to hurt, and cry, and agonize . . . let yourself have that . . . the way that you feel isn't indicative of who you really are, so hold onto what you know and not what you feel at this moment . . . give yourself time to have feelings, and time to let them pass." I have decided that feelings are real, and that's why it is important for me to acknowledge them and let myself experience them. I have also decided, though, that what "feelings" I respond to may not be real, but may be misperceptions. That is why my inner chatter is vital in helping me to be patient and to combat negative feelings that may be rooted in some dysfunctional pattern that I learned years and years ago. It has been interesting for me to realize that my emotional response is not necessarily the same thing as my inner chatter.

My anxiety attack hit Monday at noon when meeting with the active duty recruiter. During our discussion, he informed me if I were selected to go back on active duty, I would not report until 1 October, the beginning of the fiscal year. Previously I had been told I could report 1 July, but because of the financial cutbacks, the dates had all been rolled back. My troublesome inner chatter immediately took over. All I could think of was how in the hell I was going to live without money or a job. That must have crossed my mind at least a hundred times in a few seconds. The recruiter asked if I was all right, that I looked like I was in shock. I told him this news threw me totally off balance and since the board is meeting two weeks before graduation, that left me completely stressed out. I finally settled down and realized that was not that much a problem at all. Not knowing the board's decision until two weeks before graduation was the actual stressor and I again thought of the Serenity Prayer. I have done everything humanly possible for a favorable decision on my behalf and I have no control now. I will accept whatever is decided and go from there. I realized it was all right for me to be anxious about the decision and the effects it has on my future employment and I am where I need to be right now.

BEING WITH A CLIENT WITHOUT THINKING

What happened was wonderful! I got this incredible "impression" or patchwork of impressions that just floated in the air. They were sensations about feelings I was picking up. It was the kind of impression that I wanted to move with to explore more in dance therapy—to let my body tell me more about it. Or, I wanted to get out my pastels and paper and draw the colors and shapes I felt and experienced there. This overall "gestalt" gave me lots of information about the family atmosphere. It felt and smelled stale and dead like no life could still be there. The system was being stifled somewhere so I began sniffing for life in each part of the system—the daughter, the mother, but not the father. Father felt closed up and holding back. I trusted these impressions more than what the family members said and their nonverbals carried through my impressions.

In being with a client without thinking about her, I have learned to hold a large question mark about her in my mind. This keeps me from making assumptions or applying labels. In that way I am open to the mysteries and surprises presented by this unique human being and am better able to empathetically experience her world.

When I tried this, what I found was that I wasn't listening to the client, but seemed to be off in my own world. I get the feeling that I didn't perform this task as it was supposed to have been done. What did I do wrong?

DISCUSSION

Your personal response to the heroes exercise probably elicited some important values with which you attempt to inspire your own life direction. Your use of inner chatter, on the other hand, may reflect attitudes that are not always consistent with your ideal images. When you did the problematic inner chatter exercise, this discrepancy between ideals and subjective experience may have become even more obvious—perhaps even embarrassing. These differences are especially important, for they reveal to you another level of valuing, apart from your ideals. Attitudes that emerge from your inner chatter enable you to begin to construct your actual patterns of world design. Remember that world design is based upon memory and habit patterns that have survival significance for you. You built your world design identity upon beliefs, expectations, conclusions, and social reinforcements that at one time or another seemed to work for you.

Here are some common value positions shared by both students and clients alike. How many of these are key beliefs in your life?

Common Value Positions		
being safe	being in control	being nice
being perfect	being open	being understood
being right	being superior	being excited
being strong	being organized	being on the edge

The more negative versions of value positions may also be life guidelines. They include being confused, being weak, not being understood, being disliked, being out of control, being disorganized, being wrong, being outrageous, and being dull.

It is important to recognize that in describing these value positions I am not enumerating mere characteristics of people. A value position is a habitually desired state that is sought out by a person. It provides a degree of comfort and security.

The critical insight in this exercise is that you can see your emotional or physical pain as a vehicle to discover a related value position that is precious to you. Usually the pain is seen as threatening or as interfering with the valued state you would prefer.

What is a powerful realization is that your usual avowed values, or principles for living, are quite different from the experiential values that run your inner chatter and direct much of your behavior. There emerges a personal confrontation between your philosophy/religion and your subjective experience. A discomforting aspect of this exercise is sensing some of the unbecoming activities that are associated with such value positions. Even when the value position appears to be "good," such as being strong or organized, you may discover how your personal attitudes of grandiosity and the need to control are inevitably involved.

> *Grandiosity and Control*
> self-righteousness
> self-deception
> judging others (condemning)
> manipulating others
> narrowness and exclusiveness

If one prizes specific ways of being, one must exclude their opposites. If one wants to have others see one in a certain way, one must often be manipulative and self-deceptive. Grandiosity is the process of idolizing oneself, or some aspect of one's personality, as more important than other people and more important than an appreciation of life generally. The powers of both self-deception and the need to manipulate others are enormous. They are usually justified out of personal pride, a need for security, or a desire for pleasure (or, at least, less pain). While these notions are negative, and somewhat disturbing, they need to be normalized as a natural process associated with the need to become an individual and therefore establish a personal world design. We all need identities. These are based in memory and repetition.

The exercise of being with a client without thinking may shift you from the "heaviness" of world design exploration toward the "lightness" of empathic awareness. Some students find this exercise both affirming and relieving. Others find it impossible.

Just as judgment is associated with world design expression, compassion occurs when judgment of others is dispelled by means of empathy. Many students report an eye-opening experience with this exercise. What they feared to be a possible loss of control in the interview with a client resulted in a perfectly natural way of relaxing while being even more intensely related to the client. Some students report that they were pleasantly surprised to realize they have been doing this with clients now and then for some time. Others claim they are unable to stop thinking, as they are preoccupied with diagnostic considerations, goal and strategy planning, or worries about their own performance.

An interesting distinction emerges about the thinking process itself. Sometimes serious thinking is called for in an interview. This may be related to responsible, sometimes even cautionary, efforts to understand a client's behavior or expression. It may also be related to evaluating options as to what to do and how to do it in relation to the client's presenting theme of concern. At other times, thinking can be experienced in a more playful, spontaneous, almost automatic way, as when one interacts with the client a good deal of the time. Playful thinking is in keeping with the empathic state of mind. Empathy, therefore, can occur at times of inner silence or in playful thinking, wherein the focus of attention is fully with the here-and-now experiencing of the client.

With the inner chatter exercises you have begun to familiarize yourself with your survival and security operations. The exercise about heroes and heroines and the exercise having to do with empathic awareness with clients permit you to experience aspects of yourself other than protective world design. These are creative, integrative, merging functions of your person. In the next series of exercises you will explore in more detail both the survival and creative portions of your subjective experience. Do these before proceeding with Chapter 3.

Pain as the perfect place to be. During the coming week, attend to a time when you are quite frustrated (emotionally pained) by boredom, anxiety, anger, despair, or the like, or a time when you are in physical pain. As an experimental perspective, "try on" the notion that "right now, I'm in the perfect place for me to be." You may not be able to justify or explain this, only see if the idea somehow fits.

Triggers for inner chatter. Note your inner chatter, on occasion, and see if you can determine what set it off. This may stem from outside yourself or from some inner experience.

Role shifting. You will notice that you act, and often experience yourself, as different "selves" in your array of social roles: parent, spouse, professional helper, student, patient, friend, supervisor, adult son or daughter. Begin to play with these selves. Try switching one for another and see what occurs. For instance, assume your student role in place of your parent or spouse role.

Meditation through activity. The practice of "mindfulness" is the careful attention to your here-and-now actions. The tea ceremony of the Japanese is an example of a mindful activity. Choose a common daily activity (e.g., washing dishes, sweeping, making breakfast, getting dressed, showering, shaving) and do it with mindfulness. Just as sounds and breathing were your focus in meditative awareness, let the activity be the focus.

Chapter 3

PERSONAL FREEDOM

We will begin again with student responses, as shared in their personal journals, to the exercises you have just completed. In this chapter we will explore the interplay of a rather deterministic world design and the subjective experience of personal freedom.

JOURNAL RESPONSES TO EXERCISES

PAIN AS THE PERFECT PLACE TO BE

What I tried to do this time with my childhood pain about my Mother was to let it be there and be sad. Let the sadness provide a forum for my healing, in a sense, by accepting that it is okay for me to be sad and to feel how difficult it was for me. When I allowed it to be okay, I could accept myself in the present, I could allow myself to feel the pain but not be afraid of it or overwhelmed by it. It was a wonderfully freeing feeling, at last. I know the pain is still there, but I can continue to function in the present. I think the difference is that I allowed myself to not have to fix it right now. I gave myself a break from needing to have all the answers and solutions right now.

I used the perfect place exercise in a way that I would rather not have. The day after class, I fell going up stairs at the library and injured my toe and my knee. I was in a lot of pain for the rest of the day and have dealt with the aftermath all week. As soon as I was free to put a mental frame around what I was experiencing, I tried to believe that this was the perfect place for me to be. I reacted violently against that attitude. I can accept painful emotions as the perfect place for me at the moment, but I have realized from this experience that I am not willing to accept physical pain or illness. I am supposed to be healthy, and I fight ill health and pain. I believe that if I do something different, it will somehow be repaired (i.e., I can control it).

TRIGGERS FOR INNER CHATTER

Trying to grasp the birth of a thought was an amazing thing to have to do. The harder I tried, the more elusive the idea became. I know that there are times when some interaction or incident will be familiar enough to generate a memory about a past event. Sometimes that will depress me. It used to be that I would suddenly realize that I was feeling extremely depressed and had no idea why. Over the years I have realized that usually it is because I had remembered some event in which I had done or said something that I felt was extremely stupid and I was feeling stupid all over again. I have so many memories of things that I have done that I bitterly regret doing and they do tend to surface. However, it seems that the older I get, the less that happens. I realize that I am talking about a pattern in my life that makes up part of my world design. MEMORIES bring up past IMAGES which create the PROBLEM, which is depression. My INNER CHATTER must first work to identify the thought process and then begin to refute the validity of it. The fact is that I feel inferior to a great many people and I don't like feeling inferior. I spend a lot of time overachieving because that somehow helps to make me feel less inferior—for a time.

The triggers, I think, are when I let in someone else's ideas and give them more power than my own ideas. I somehow distrust my ideas or feelings totally, or at least I allow my inner chatter to express this, even though the rest of me might not believe my inner chatter. The danger of this situation is that I let the inner chatter go on almost unconsciously, which tears down my own confidence in myself until I notice it. I think I need to work on giving myself positive input with my inner chatter, or at least consciously counteracting that unconscious need to put myself down.

It seems that often when I'm experiencing feelings, whatever they may be, the inner chatter comes in, which makes it difficult to just be with those feelings. Some of this chatter is very "other" focused, such as feeling good or feeling lousy about how others perceived me. I realize then how controlled I am by societal forces and feel like if I could get rid of these and therefore experience myself outside my usual sense of self, I could have a more keen experience.

ROLE SHIFTING

The exercise in role shifting produces surprising reactions for those who try it. Many do not attempt it, fearing the risk of embarrassment.

A basic premise here is that we are all "multiple personalities" of a sort. The most obvious expression of these varied images (or personalities) is in the roles we take in differing situations. The shifting of roles (being a student instead of a parent when with one's child, for example) makes obvious what otherwise goes unnoticed. If the student is lacking awareness of the differences, the other person with whom he or she is performing the role change will commonly react in a different manner.

In the three exercises discussed above, you have seen your world design identity as a powerful actor. The "perfect place" effort finds your security images protesting, rebelling, and demanding through inner chatter. With the triggers observed, you see that your identity is not only a reactor to pain, but can actively take charge of your awareness and direct your energies, often as a result of some quite ordinary occurrence. A sign, song, chance encounter, or even an arising sensation or emotion may open the floodgates of memory; your chatter is off and running. The role-shifting task reveals how automatic a process your security image-making activity can be—so automatic that you are usually not even aware of it in terms of inner chatter. Yet if you consider altering that role-taking process, you immediately threaten a set of assumptions, and your inner chatter busily contends with your new intentions: "Become a student with my kid? Not on your life!"

How does this self-restricting process play itself out with your clients? Consider this: The more one is attempting to play out a "professional" role with a client, the more likely it will be that the client will play out a "patient" role. This can be a detriment to the counseling process and is commonly the cause of unnecessarily long-term, overly dependent worker-client relationships. This should not be taken to imply that clients should never be seen on a long-term basis, but rather that this sometimes results from the need of the worker more than from the need of the client. If the client wants to manipulate you so as to maintain his or her own sense of security, then the more predictable your role behavior is, the more easily you are manipulated. On the other hand, if you wish to sidestep the manipulative moves of a client, it is useful to not be so attached to your own prescribed professional role.

Here we are faced with the question of subjective freedom. How can you detach from your world design as it assumes the guise of a counselor? Chapter 8 will address this question in some detail. For the moment it is enough to say that this freedom is sometimes described by master therapists in terms such as lightness, humor, compassion, and self-awareness. Carlos Castaneda's popularized description of a similar freeing activity was described in *Journey to Ixtlan* (1972) as "creating a fog" and as "losing personal history."

MEDITATION THROUGH ACTIVITY

The meditation exercise you did in Chapter 1 suggested the use of here-and-now awareness as a means of detaching from world design demands and preoccupations. Two of the exercises in Chapter 2, pain as the perfect place to be and meditation through activity, provide further experiences that elaborate upon this process of how detachment occurs.

The perfect place exercise is a no-lose learning situation. You, like many students, may have been surprised that the exercise produced sudden relief or understanding, or diminished inner chatter immediately. On the other hand, you may have found the exercise puzzling or of no benefit. Even so, you probably could specify a value position that was being threatened by the pain encountered. If this occurred, consider this question: If that was not the perfect place, where should you have been (what experience would you have preferred) instead? What makes you think that your preference is correct—more right than what was being presented to you by your life? You may have a clue, here, as to how your own personal grandiosity operates.

When you affirm your pain as the perfect place to be and experience the truth of this strange assertion, you immediately experience an inner freedom. You are not bothering yourself with your usual complaints and protests. Your energy is freed for other uses.

David Reynolds (1984) uses meditation through activity as a key form of teaching in his version of Morita therapy, a therapy developed originally in Japan and based upon some premises of Zen Buddhism. He demonstrates an interesting use of awareness: Accept your disturbed feelings and related thoughts as they arise, *and do what needs doing.* This is not a new version of "the power of positive thinking"—you are not trying to suppress feelings and brainwash yourself in an upbeat fashion. You accept troubling feelings, pain, and so on, and do some activity with the full focus of your attention on the activity itself. Here you shift your attention from self-preoccupation to how you are currently being addressed by life, in terms of responsibilities, tasks, expectations, and challenges.

The pain you may commonly experience while interviewing a client will take the forms of anxiety over not knowing what to do, being puzzled as to the meaning of a client's complaints and behavior, worry about what your supervisor has said or will say, troubling emotions aroused, as well as worries over personal life events that are totally unconnected with your client. One way of conceptualizing this inner process of reaction to pain is illustrated in Figure 3.1.

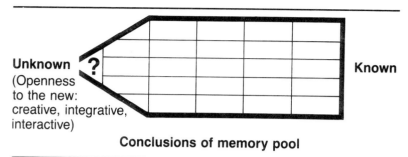

Conclusions of memory pool

Figure 3.1 Experiencing Freedom

The rocket ship form represents the individual's own world design, characterized by a gridiron of attitudes, beliefs, images, and conclusions based in accumulated memories. Being human, however, we must realize that none of us is a fixed identity of predictable reactions; rather, we are always involved in a process of change. The open tip of the rocket shape shown in the figure represents potential here-and-now openness to change. These changes result both from our interactions with the daily changing environment and from the creative-integrative process that is continually going on inside us, often outside of our conscious awareness. New potentials, limitations, and understandings are being unraveled or generated. Freedom is experienced as we allow this emerging uniqueness into our here-and-now awareness.

The "openness to the new" that occurs with you and a client is found in that unknown experience of the here and now. In this very moment of encountering your client is found the possibility for freedom, for stepping outside your own judgments, conclusions, and expectations. The unknown, of course, feels risky because one has no idea as to where it will lead. You had such moments when you did the Chapter 1 exercise on being with a client without thinking.

Freedom, then, is experienced in those moments, not unlike peak experiences, when we do not use our inner chatter and automatic behavior patterns to interfere with the spontaneous creative-integrative process between ourselves and our surrounding world. We are speaking of that existential moment, that wonder of the poet and artist, that rhythmic action of the juggler and fine athlete. We embrace the flow of life as change and surprise.

The meditation through activity exercise is often an eye-opener. Actions commonly perceived of as drudgery and repetitious (such as washing dishes or washing the car) are suddenly experienced in a meaningful fashion. This is not a conceptualized meaning but rather an

experienced one. Why are dull actions now felt to be otherwise? What
has changed? You have freed yourself from the usual subliminal conclusions you use to take the sense of wonder and engagement out of
your daily awareness.

Here are two student responses to that exercise:

> I have probably done moving meditation in the past, bike riding. The
> focusing allowed me to better do one aspect of my riding that needs work,
> and that is to relax. I'm not always able to relax when I want to and was
> able to get in touch with how that felt and could repeatedly do it. I did not
> have the problem as before, with extraneous thoughts coming in. I realized
> while thinking about this exercise that my cycling is one place where I've
> had some peak experiences, by being so in tune to my movement and my
> bike's movement and experiencing an incredible efficiency of motion that
> was a real peak experience.

> My partner attempted to focus on her shower routine. She had difficulty
> since every move had become automatic. She did go step-by-step through
> portions of her routine. Making certain all toiletries needed were available
> (i.e., shampoo, soap, etc.). She then realized just how involved one's body
> is in the showering process. She began to think of the difficulty a person
> with no or without the use of arms and legs would have in doing something
> we take so for granted. She also had inner chatter creep in throughout her
> process. Things like what to do at work, home, and school today, disrupt-
> ing her concentration.

The following are two important exercises that will enable you to
explore further the nature of freedom, as discussed in this chapter. The
first involves your relationship with a client; the second requires you to
intensify your experience with meditation.

Pain of a client as the perfect place to be. Just as you did with
yourself, now let yourself experience the physical or emotional pain of
a client as the perfect place for him or her to be. You should not attempt
this with a client unless you experienced an "appropriate fit" when you
did this with yourself. You are not asked to share your view with the
client, but simply to experience the client as being in the "perfect
place."

Sitting meditation. Sit for a period of 20 minutes in meditation. You
may use sounds, breath counting, or some word (mantra) or image as
your focal point of attention. You are not expected to stop thinking but
simply to lessen the pressure of thoughts, so you do not pursue them in
your usual manner.

Now, in preparation for the next chapter, select a personal problem
of concern—one in which you can see yourself as having some part (that

is, the problem is not completely caused by someone else). You may not be sure you are prepared to change this troubling problem. In the next chapter you will have an opportunity to study the problem in some depth, just as you may later do with a client's concern. Your very study will help you decide if this is the time to do something different about your problem or not.

What you will find different about this way of problem study is that the problem will not be seen as some unwanted foreign intruder in your life. Rather, your problem will be seen as a helpful companion—a perfectly natural expression of your world design!

Students, fearing the unknown, tend to overuse categorization of their clients. They mistakenly believe that a category explains the client and prescribes some useful procedure. They end up "treating" the category at the expense of the client. Categorization occurs not only in the use of diagnostic labels, but in all types of stereotyping of clients (client as addict, racist, abuser, chauvinist, liar, and so on). One of the most common reinforcers of this process is the "sophisticated" jargon bandied about among students and professionals.

Chapter 4

THE PERSON IS NOT THE CATEGORY

How did you do with viewing the client's pain as the perfect place for him or her to be? Some students find this more difficult than when applying the "perfect place" to themselves. Others find it easier to do this with clients than for themselves. In either case, common themes usually emerge from student discussions of this exercise that may be helpful for you.

First, there is a challenge concerning the appropriateness of the word *perfect*. Many students believe words such as *only, best,* or *natural* would be more accurate. There is no need to dispute word usage here so long as you grasp the essence of the exercise: acceptance and affirmation (valuing) of one's experiences, however painful. The message to a client is this: This is your truth; this is your life; "be it" for now rather than protest it.

Did you experience a realization of enormous relief at not having to rescue the client? You do not *have* to make the client "feel better." Some students even state that they feel greater empathy, an increase in intensity, when they are willing simply to be with the client in his or her pain without attempting to change it. Those with field placements in hospice settings compare this exercise with what they must learn in responding to dying patients. Many students report surprise at seeing how clients begin to affirm their own strength when the students do not try to "problem solve."

You may struggle with the same question with clients as you did in relation to yourself. If the client should not be experiencing what he or she is experiencing, what should the client be experiencing instead? The

40

answer to this question (should not have pain, should be happy, for example) leads to the unsettling questions: Why? How do you know that is best for the client?

On occasion a student will relate this exercise to the religious concept: doing God's will versus doing one's own will. Other students may speak of a similar idea in nonreligious terms: honoring the total life process as it is now occurring versus wanting it your own way. How have you conceptualized this experience?

How did you do with the meditation effort?

Sitting meditation is a challenge and surprise for students who have never before practiced meditation. Sitting in silence for 20 minutes and doing this alone is far more difficult for most than meditation through activity. In sitting, with eyes closed or focused upon one spot, there are few distractions to occupy the senses and the mind. Inner chatter intensifies as it seeks to rescue the self from the threatening void of momentary silence. Yet, despite the discomfort, students often are able to pinpoint at least three important uses for this exercise.

First, meditation provides a way of relaxing when one is tense. It even helps one detach from the flurry of worry related to plans for the day or reflections on the previous day. One can experience oneself in a simple and direct fashion as "just being" apart from expectations, conclusions, comparisons, and the like. In this detached state one may feel more "centered" and less dominated or controlled by outside forces. Beginning the day with meditation is very different from beginning with the morning news and a review of one's schedule and preparations.

Second, meditation can be therapeutic. Those who have practiced sitting meditation for some time report that as one is gradually more and more successful in "letting go" of thoughts there occurs an appearance of "unfinished business" in one's awareness. Memories surface that had been repressed, along with a sense of needing to resolve a situation or at least learn from it.

Third, similar to the appearance of unfinished business, one also notices a natural integrative or creative process occurring. As inner chatter lessens, you may discover increased clarity as to "what needs doing" in your present life situation. You may experience the meaning of being addressed by the world. You may also sense your best and unique potential response to this address. Life is a dialogue at such moments, just as described by Martin Buber (Friedman, 1960, chap. 14).

Now consider this question: Can a change in your conscious process effect change in the world about you? This idea is the way teachers of Eastern wisdom, such as Krishnamurti, respond to questions about social change. The idea also hits at the heart of the problem of countertransference. Could a "detached caring" be applied both to control manipulations of clients and to social action and political power struggles? This will be discussed at more length in Chapter 7. For now it is sufficient to see that to the extent you lessen the inner chatter defining your world design, the less susceptible you will be to the expectations of others built upon their stereotype of you. An added benefit of the "centered" state that may result (for a while, at least) from meditation is that your attentiveness to your surroundings is greatly enhanced. You therefore have more to which you can respond and in which you can engage yourself.

JOURNAL RESPONSES TO EXERCISES

PAIN OF A CLIENT AS THE PERFECT PLACE TO BE

I was feeling pretty anxious and concerned about a young new client who had missed an appointment the week before. She's very ambivalent about coming in to see me, and I was spending a lot of time anticipating this week's session, wondering how to "hook-in" with her. My first attempts at letting go of my worries and anxiety and trying to just live the moment didn't work. I found myself thinking about it just as much as I had before and, in addition, being frustrated that my homework experiment would be a flop. As I tried again to let go of the situation and to go with the flow, I found myself relaxing a bit and saying "It's not all in my control anyway. I can't predict how this client will deal with her thoughts and feelings and I don't need to worry about them." This was not a very easy exercise, and yet the end result was quite positive. When I finally quit trying to plan the interaction between myself and this girl I became aware of my own anxiety about the situation in a much different way than I was experiencing it before. I realized that my feelings had to do with anxiety around beginning the relationship and were probably very similar to ones she was experiencing. Anyway, the perfect opportunity to raise this as a possible concern occurred within the first few minutes of our session, and I felt very comfortable in bringing it up. Much to my surprise the client shared with me some of her own feelings about beginning and we simply talked about it together.

It is harder for me to experience a CLIENT IN PAIN as the perfect place for that person to be than to experience my own pain within that context. I think this is true because I have a degree of control over my response to pain. Yet, I have no control over the client's response, so how can I judge it as the "perfect place"? My client seems to have had such intense and tremendous pain that she has shut down around it, and I ask myself how being shut down can be the perfect place. Although I can be with her in her pain and allow her to experience it while I am simply "a presence," it is hard to understand such terrific pain as being the perfect place for her. Yet I know that judgment must be hers, and not mine.

SITTING MEDITATION

What a wonderful gift—"mandated" meditation. Allowed me to nurture myself. No difficulty letting go of thoughts . . . they drift away easily. No resistance. A deep welcoming of the sea visualization, a sense of being the wave washing in and out, in and out. Timeless, soothing, universal. Difficulty with sound focus as my mind skated away to a visual focus.

Meditation is something I've wanted to do for years, thought I would get something out of, and have little idea of what it is. During my attempt at meditation, for really the first time ever, extraneous thoughts kept coming in, only briefly as I was able to go back to concentrating on my breathing. I found myself frustrated over not knowing what I was supposed to get out of it. I have become real aware over the past two weeks of how important this is to me. Unstructured situations cause anxiety for me. I'm not comfortable with just taking the experience for what it's going to be to me, but feel a need for at least vague guidelines of what my role is or what's possible in a situation.

PROBLEM EXPLORATION EXERCISES

Now we are ready to address the personal problem you have selected for purposes of exploration. The model for problem study we will utilize is compatible with most theoretical orientations that seek to explain the dynamics, or cause-effect elements, of client problems (Krill, 1986, chap. 4). It maintains the social work perspective of emphasizing interpersonal relationships and other social forces of the client's present life situation.

situation:	dual focus
	past and present relationships
problem:	specificity
	mutuality
person:	normalization
	world design images

What is emphasized in this model is the lack of any need for diagnostic classification, although one may add that if one so desires. The point here is that one is primarily interested in understanding those

aspects of a client's worldview that are problem related. It is the
uniqueness of the person's world design that is stressed, rather than its
similarities to those of other clients. Furthermore, the person is normalized in relation to his or her problem rather than pathologized—"When
you look at yourself and how you conclude you must deal with the
world, it is no wonder you have a symptom like this!" Since each of us
creates his or her own world design, who is to say that one is better than
another? Each person must find his or her own way of evaluating the
rightness of his or her world design. For some this is determined by a
simple assessment: Is it workable? There are no problem-free
worldviews. For others there will be some image of maturity, happiness,
holiness, or security by which they will measure themselves. It is not
the counselor's role to belittle or denigrate such images. One seeks to
understand these images and point out the natural consequences (sometimes problematic) that are related to living according to them. How
one came to develop one's present world design is of no special importance, except as a means of imparting interest and understanding so as
to join with the client and lessen one's own tendencies to stereotype.
So there needs be no great emphasis at discovering or "uncovering"
forgotten traumas, secrets, and horrors.

What is of great importance is clarifying how the client's world
design is currently operating and tied in with the problems of concern.
It is presumptuous to believe one could understand a client's world
design in its full complexity, and this is not necessary. The worker needs
to understand only how specific images or conclusions of the client's
world design are producing or at least maintaining problems.

The problems themselves are studied in detail, in terms of onset,
effects on life-style, involvement of other people, efforts used to
change, times and places of occurrence, history of similar problems in
the past or within the family and how these were worked out, and so on.
A guideline for problem study follows generally the areas used for
problem exploration in the imagination exercise you will be using on
yourself.

The mutuality sphere of problem study has to do with a clear agree-
ment between client and worker as to what is the problem of concern.
Here one must be especially careful not to seduce clients into believing
that some "deep problem" underlies the presenting symptom. While this
will sometimes be the case, it is essential that the client fully realizes
the truth of this formulation for him- or herself. The client must own
the problem and must not be seeking to please the worker.

The situation emphasizes the dual focus of social work thinking. This dual focus states that the problem does not exist solely within the psyche of the individual, nor is it solely the fault of environmental circumstance. The problem lies in the interface, the engagement (or lack thereof) between the person and the environment. The situation provides the details as to the person's "being in the world." To understand the person one must look first at the person's behavior. What roles does this person take in relation to others and to activities? How have these changed over time? What patterns and habits have persisted over time? The term *situation* refers both to the present and to significant past events in the person's life. It refers also to the future—toward what purposes or goals is the person committed and why? The careful assessment of the situation also reveals the most useful information for eventually moving the client toward change, namely, the resources of other people and of former experiences in the client's life.

Both assessment areas of situation and problem study are no doubt familiar to you from your learning in other classes and in field supervision. What may be new here is the idea of understanding a client's world design as a result of the situation and problem study.

You will need to experience the operation of your own world design in relation to your selected problem. Here is a summary of the elements of world design that you will be exploring in relation to your own problem:

world design images ←	problem related	{	attitudes, beliefs cause-effect conclusions emotions empowering memories body use activity use roles with others

Do not worry at this point about being unclear as to the meaning of the concept of world design. The two exercises will provide you with the data necessary to construct relevant aspects of your world design. The concept will clarify itself. Read the following directions and then close your eyes and do the first exercise.

Begin by noticing your present feelings, thoughts, and points of bodily tension. Then attend to your breathing and follow it, allowing it to flow more deeply. Visualize yourself in a situation wherein you are experiencing your problem.

Now, first notice any bodily reactions in your visualization. What sensations, facial expressions, gestures do you discover? Press on—what more of any of these are generated in your imagery?

Next, what emotions occur in your imagery? Are there others?

You will also discover inner chatter of attitudes and beliefs about your problem, and even some conclusions as to why you have such a problem. Stay with this, as your visualization has much to say to you in this regard.

What reactions do others have to your problem? Who gets most involved with your problem? Who is most upset by it? Why do they believe you have this problem?

How do you use your activities and interests to help you manage this problem?

Finally, what memory surfaces for you? Let any early memory appear; don't force one. What does it reveal to you?

Now write down the data that you discovered in relation to each phase of your exploration.

When doing this exercise be sure to give yourself ample time, at least 15 minutes. The spirit of this exercise should be one of free association, not rational reflection. You are seeking to surface an array of details that you will later integrate for yourself.

The next exercise is best done with a partner who will ask you a series of simple questions. You can do it alone, pressing yourself with the same questions, but you will miss out on the powerful interpersonal impact of the exercise. Again, you should write down the results of this effort in your journal. This exercise will provide further data that, when combined with the above imagination exercise, will enhance your understanding of relevant aspects of your world design.

Begin by stating your problem in a short, succinct manner. The questioner then asks: "What payoffs or rewards do you get from your problem?" Answer this spontaneously, without worry as to the importance or accuracy of your statement. The questioner should not respond to your comment, but should simply repeat the question. Each time you answer, the question is posed to you once more, until you cannot answer with any new responses.

The questioner then asks: "What pains or miseries result from your problem?" Proceed with the same cycle of spontaneous answers and repeated question as you did before.

You will notice that your free-association answers to the question of payoffs may include excuses, self-justifications, self-pleasuring, and attention from others. Your answers to the pain and misery question may include trouble with self-esteem, with integrity, and with quality of relationships.

Having completed these two exercises, you now have the challenging task of answering this question: How is your problem a perfectly natural expression of your world design? This can be a discomforting puzzler for you, because we have learned to view our problems more as foreign intruders than as helpful companions. Once you appreciate a problem as a helpful companion you will appreciate the concept of client resistance.

In my classes I demonstrate the nature of world design in the following way. I ask for a student volunteer to share a problem and situation before the class in response to my probing questions. Following this interview, which usually takes 30 to 40 minutes, I ask the class to make guesses as to what conclusions and images are important to the student's world design. The student interviewed need only agree or disagree with the speculations set forth by the class. At the conclusion of this exchange between the class and the interviewed student, I will summarize the elements of world design the student has owned as reality.

This role play demonstrates clearly for all students not only how world design speculation results from the situation-problem data, but also how the worker needs to check out the validity of such speculation with the client. The method of interviewing pursues situation data in considerable detail before even inquiring about the problem. Students are surprised to notice how much they can already surmise about world design images before ever hearing about the problem. The discussion, then, of the problem helps observers focus on the aspects of world design directly related to symptoms of concern. Here is a journal response from a student who volunteered to share her situation and problem in a classroom interview:

Ouch! is my overall response to the experience of being interviewed and being so vulnerable before so many of my peers. I consciously chose to volunteer because I wanted to work on the problem with my response to my client. (I'm sure there was an element of grandiosity in it, too.) I was emotionally exhausted when we finished. As the class members were telling me about my worldview, I wanted to take notes because I was sure there would be elements of my blind spot in what they were saying, and I knew I wouldn't remember everything. However, there was very little in what was said that was surprising.

Students commonly express appreciation for this form of assessment because it avoids the imposition of categorical thinking. It seems to

flow naturally from the details of the person's life and the worldview
assumptions around which they build a life-style. There is no need to
use jargon to explain the dynamics of a client. Students contrast this
approach with what appears to them to be a facile and smug objectifi-
cation of clients in many agencies. Read the following journal responses
to the problem exploration exercises, and then evaluate your own data
and write a brief description of how your personal problem reflects or
expresses certain aspects of your own world design. What patterns,
beliefs, conclusions, and expectations that you regularly utilize are
involved in maintaining your problem? What would you need to give
up if you were going to change, if you were going to deal with this
problem in a new fashion?

JOURNAL RESPONSES

PROBLEM EXPLORATION

> Dyad exercise of working on a problem with questions was helpful to get
> a better view of the problem for me. It was interesting to me how easy it
> is to miss a key benefit of keeping the problem—how easy it is to be blind
> to what's really driving the problem. I think looking at pains of self-esteem
> and damage to self-expression helped us both focus more on how the
> problem was holding us back.

> Since last class, I have been thinking a lot about world design. I became
> a bit obsessed with it and wished that I had volunteered for the interview
> in class. I tried answering the same questions you asked the volunteer,
> wrote them down and thought about what it all meant with regard to how
> I view the world. My own opinions came through, but I did manage to
> figure out a couple of things. I do expect perfection from other people
> (particularly friends) but I don't expect it of myself. I can always find
> some excuse for whatever it is that *I* do wrong. The things that bug me
> most about others are those characteristics that I display as well. Also,
> I am very proud about my independence, and the fact that I've made it
> alone most of my life. Yet this independence translates into loneliness as
> well. I'm not sure why I remain so alone, but it's funny that "loneliness"
> was the problem I used for the profits and pains exercise we did in class
> a while back. When I was asked how I benefited from my problem, I was
> about to say "nothing." Then I saw that a "benefit" was the safety of
> remaining unhurt. I also gain my privacy and not having to "give" of
> myself—although in the long run, this is troublesome.

> I found all of the exercises this time quite revealing and informative about
> my own worldview and how entrenched it probably is. The payoffs and
> pains exploration of a problem seemed to indicate for both my partner and

I that we were often fully invested in seeing the problem as "out there" and not as a direct expression of who we are. There was some security in keeping the problem. It seemed much easier to "hug" the problem than to consider the possibility of altering my worldview! For the most part, the difficulty seems to be largely in even *comprehending* my worldview— getting detached enough to see it for what it is. As I indicated when you did the interview with me in class, it would have been much harder (probably useless) to try to answer the question "What is your worldview?" directly, than to demonstrate it (as I obviously did so well) and also to *acknowledge* it after hearing it presented back to me from the perspective of the other class members.

Somehow in this whole process, my problem, which before the exercise had made no sense to me at all, began to make more sense. Instead of having the view that it was unfair to me and saying constantly to myself, "I don't deserve this problem," I began to understand the complicated processes throughout my life that led up to this series of events. I realized the role I have accepted all my life and I know now why my present dilemma has been forthcoming for some time. I'm not saying that I believe that I "deserve" these consequences. "Deserving" this painful situation would mean that I am still of the mind-set that it's a cruel situation. I no longer see it as "cruel," but rather as a natural occurrence of events which reflect my continual life processes. In other words, the constant manner in which I have viewed and lived my life in general has brought me to my present circumstance. My world design made it inevitable that I would be where I am right now. After making this discovery about myself and my problem situation, I was able to take a good look at significant others in my life that I had been blaming for my problem.

NEW EXERCISE

There is one new exercise you need to complete before proceeding to the next chapter. It is related to the problem exploration and world design study you did here, although the connection may not be immediately apparent.

Guilt inventory. This exercise is similar to the fourth step in the 12-step program of Alcoholics Anonymous: List important areas of guilt that have occurred over the span of your life. Doing this list in 5- or 10-year segments is helpful. Having accomplished your list, distinguish between what you consider realistic guilt and what you believe to be neurotic, or unrealistic, guilt.

Chapter 5

GUILT AND ITS RESOLUTION

You should have completed two tasks by this time: conceptualization of your problem as an expression of your world design, and development of a guilt inventory. Guilt inevitably accompanies world design and most problems that stem from this. In this chapter we shall explore these connections and seek to understand guilt as a positive force rather than a negative, unwanted pain.

How did you respond to your guilt inventory? Did you do it? If not, why not? Could you separate realistic from unrealistic guilt? How did you determine the difference? Was this a depressing or annoying experience for you? Why? Did it feel like some sort of trap or prison? Guilt has certainly acquired a bad name, as we commonly even dislike our own actions when they are motivated by guilt. Yet when we observe others who claim to be guilt free, are we really impressed by their lifestyle? Too often their excuses and justifications betray self-deceptions. An irritating self-centeredness often characterizes their attitudes. Why have saints traditionally been said to be the most guilt discriminating of all people? Is it because they have allowed themselves to be dominated by some dogmatic religious hierarchy? Or is guilt sensitivity a characteristic of the highest levels of human experience? Should you be reassuring your clients that they need not be guilty because they are somehow not responsible? Most clients seem to seek this reassurance in either direct or indirect ways from their counselors.

The subject of guilt is highly controversial. A number of students avow that they are without any realistic guilt. Freud's interpretation of guilt as a neurotic symptom is reassuring to them. Other students seem so plagued by the pain of their personal continuing guilt that they fear the guilt inventory exercise as "too painful." Mowrer's (1961) conclusion that the basis of most emotional problems is unresolved realistic guilt provides an overwhelming specter for guilt-driven students. The majority of students seem to accept some guilt as natural and reality based, and some guilt as a disguise of sorts and therefore not clearly realistic.

In contrast to Freud, theologian Paul Tillich (1952) speaks of guilt as ontological, that is, as an inevitable aspect of what it means to be human. Hobart Mowrer (1961), a psychologist from a Sullivanian background, claimed that realistic guilt underlies all emotional problems. What appears as neurotic, unrealistic guilt is simply a deceptive and diversionary tactic (pp. 81-102). One prefers to connect real guilt feelings with false or antiquated issues so as to gain reassurance from one's significant others, friends, and therapist. The first goal to be accomplished, according to Mowrer, is to help a client clarify the nature of his or her realistic guilt. Realistic guilt is related to not being true to one's own values (integrity), denying the need for guiding values (avoidance), or breaking agreements with others or outright hurting them. Mowrer's integrity therapy process focuses next upon what people could do to resolve their real guilt.

An apparently opposing point of view is that of Krishnamurti. While Mowrer emphasizes Western religious thinking (confession, amends, reconciliation) in his understanding of and resolution of guilt, Krishnamurti (1971) represents Eastern wisdom. Krishnamurti would state that what we call guilt is regret for choices that we do not really have to begin with. Our behavior stems from our limited and rather fixed identity (world design). If one could have done some regrettable action differently, one would have. The repetitive power of our world design is so strong, our choices are determined for us. This sounds much like the Freudian unconscious. Krishnamurti goes on, however, to point out that we all have one choice, and this is how we use our awareness at any given moment. We may use it to activate and submerge ourselves in the habitual processes of our world design. We may also use it to step outside of any identification with this world design process. Krishnamurti speaks of this as seeing things (including our subjective reactions) quite simply, as they are, without evaluative thought. This perspective is not so different from that of those Western religious writers who state that only one choice is of any consequence: the choice between doing God's will or doing one's own.

Another perspective is that of Frederick Perls. When a client complained of guilt, Perls (1969) would suggest that he or she explore it

through a series of sentences beginning with "I resent . . . " (p. 48).
Following this elaboration on resentment, Perls would request the
person do another series, this time using "I demand . . . ." So, for Perls,
what lay behind guilt was resentment and what underlay resentment
were hidden demands. Now this has the appearance of pure psychology,
apart from religion. Yet, what do demands imply? Grandiosity: I know
best what you must do. Camilla Anderson (1970), another psychologist,
has posited that most emotional problems, wherein there is no physical
component, result from disguised grandiosity. She interprets helplessness, depression, resentment, and the like as variations on the theme of
grandiosity. And what do we find to be the Judeo-Christian definition
of sin? Grandiosity. One puts oneself, rather than God, at the center of
the world. Nature, possessions, and other people are used to accomplish
one's personal ends. Grandiosity is maintained by pride, the antithesis
of religious humility.

You have, no doubt, already noted how self-deceptions and manipulations are involved in your own use of world design. We hide parts of
ourselves from our awareness. We blame others for what we refuse to
own about ourselves. We maneuver others to see us in ways that flatter
our self-images. We pretend to be victims of our problems, seeing
symptoms as foreign intruders. We excuse our failures to change in
ways that we have concluded will benefit us. Deception of oneself and
deception of others results in guilt. One is hiding from the truth.

Realistic guilt is directive. Some action is called for. One must
commit oneself to changing some troubling pattern. One must make
amends to someone who has been hurt. One must shift the very use one
makes of one's energy or awareness. One must reclarify values or
agreements. One must shift the use of a behavior from selfish to
nonselfish ends. One must seek forgiveness.

When guilt seems unrealistic or "murky," one must first explore it in
detail. What might one be realistically guilty about, given one's world
design patterns? Here one may need the feedback of significant others,
or a professional helper who is skilled in detailed exploration of one's
situation. In relation to unattached or murky guilt, what resentments and
then demands can be brought into awareness?

Religion is commonly blamed for the origin and reinforcement of
much childhood guilt. If it wasn't a righteous relative, it was the nuns
at parochial school or the rigid minister, priest, or rabbi. The exploration
of guilt is a key predecessor to the discussion in Chapter 8 on the subject
of religion.

Here is an exercise aimed at improving your own sensitivity to the
guilt-producing process of your own inner chatter. Utilizing categories

developed in relation to the thought of Krishnamurti, you may *study the specific use of your inner chatter.* There are three categories: time-binding, ego power, and partializing. These are ways by which we fortify, solidify, and secure our world design in a continuing manner, which impairs our possibility of freedom. Time-binding involves the use of memories, anticipations, and efforts to maintain a sense of continuity of the self (the ongoing free-associative process that avoids inner silences). Ego power involves reflections about oneself as a stable entity; as an owner of material objects, forms of nature (land, plants, pets), and even people viewed as possessions. Ego power also operates when we are preoccupied with ourselves as mentor or ego-ideal and source of self-pride, and as power expanding wherein one is fascinated by one's own development and self-actualization. Partializing is a victimizing process promoting the sense of separation of self and others. It includes the use of prejudices, comparisons, longing for others seen as opposite to oneself, competition, and seeking after what one believes to be lacking (Dhopeshwarkar, 1967, pp. 80-115).

There is a second exercise that is far more familiar to you in terms of either producing guilt or seeking to avoid guilt. Be sure to do this one before reading the next chapter.

Change a behavior pattern. Change a troubling or annoying pattern of behavior. This may be related to the problem you studied earlier, although this is not necessary. You may use any simple habit pattern, such as getting up later or earlier, being on time, or altering some eating or drinking pattern. Do your best to make this an effort of your own, something that will be a benefit to you, rather than doing this simply as an assignment. Maintain the change for one week. Especially important for you is to note the inner chatter related to this exercise—the conflicts, struggles, self-pity, and so on. Note any other changes in your environment that occur in response to your change effort.

JOURNAL RESPONSES TO EXERCISE

GUILT INVENTORY

Guilt has been an important influence in my life, and I've struggled for years to get a handle on its power. At times I can control the extent to which I feel guilt, but at other times it seems to control me almost as if it were a force outside of myself that pushes or pulls me in different directions. It's so amazing to me how "guilt" (usually neurotic guilt) can either suppress creativity, spontaneity, and the adventuresome spirit, or it can be the force that drives you and stimulates these same things. I personally like the idea that realistic guilt can lead a person to something constructive. Or that by getting in touch with yourself through your guilt you can find ways of going back to a painful or confusing situation and repair it. This is how I try to manage my guilt. It becomes part of my conscience. As I sort through different situations using my inner chatter, I try to pinpoint the experience of my guilty feelings. Then I continue to process the real or experienced situation while substituting those things that I goofed up or mishandled, or the things that I missed altogether with thoughts and images of how I would have done them differently. Those things that I cannot change, I find a way to reconcile myself with. But, the experiences that involve something ongoing or current, I try to find ways of repairing. This has been extremely important in my life and has given me much strength. It's a wonderful feeling to be able to say, "I changed something about myself that I didn't particularly like," or "I repaired a negative situation with someone I felt out of touch with or angry with or distant from." This can be an extremely humbling experience, one that very often involves some form of personal struggle in order to work it through. But I am usually aware of a kind of growthful feeling inside that I experience whenever I work through guilt and resolve a conflict. It's funny, but immediately following an experience of this sort, is when I feel closest to God and more alive and in touch with other people. It somehow cleanses me and restores faith and gives me strength to be the kind of person I want to be. Perhaps it's a feeling of self-forgiveness that we discussed in class. Once I can forgive or reconcile myself to myself, then I can reach out to others and get beyond my own needs. Oftentimes I find that I need other people to help me in my struggle for self-forgiveness or to resolve guilt. Not just because they might be reassuring or forgiving, but because they will be accepting and supportive of me in my struggle.

In looking at my guilt inventory I realize that throughout my life, guilt has usually been evoked in me because of some words or deed of mine that have affected another person. Often those acts or words were expressed in the passion of a moment without real thought or intent. I also have a second type of guilt which I am less comfortable with. This is a guilt which I became aware of at an early age, and it was rooted in my belief that I was different . . . it was guilt born of the fact that I thought I might be gay. It was guilt derived from my "knowing," through the teachings of my parents and church, that being gay was probably the most wretched thing that one could be. It was probably an "unforgivable sin" . . . I had such terrific guilt over this—over who I was—that I tried desperately to deny it—then change it—then hide it (even from myself). This type of guilt, which was experienced because of my very identity, was one of the most painful feelings that I have ever experienced. It began to leave me when I finally came to love myself, just as I am. When this happened I didn't require as much approval from others. It's refreshing for me to note that in some ways my patterns of guilt have changed. I no longer create guilt within myself for who I am—Who I am is who I am! It is an honest expression of myself, which is something to be proud of. A few weeks ago, when I was journaling, I realized that I had created distance between myself and other people by hiding parts of myself that I thought "they" would not approve of. In light of this, it really is something positive to be willing to risk expressing who I am. I do still experience guilt when I act in a way that is selfish or unfair to someone else. I think that guilt is healthy, though, because it helps me to know how I want to behave, and what behavior I want to work on changing. Taking action to change my own behavior is an important part of alleviating guilt for me, and so too is asking the person whom I have "wronged" for forgiveness. This owning of my behavior and taking responsibility for it allows me to forgive myself and release feelings of guilt.

I have learned when I am being unrealistic and when the guilt is realistic. I am fairly good at letting go of unrealistic guilt. The realistic guilt is usually in response to a breach of my value system, especially when it involves behavior toward other people. For the realistic guilt which is unresolved, private confession has become a tool which allows me to accept God's forgiveness and to forgive myself. That has helped me let go of things that otherwise might haunt me and keep me from getting on with my life.

In preparing for the theory complexities of the next chapter, I would like you to reflect upon your work with clients. How do you respond to resistant clients? Do you blame the client, yourself, or your theory? Given the many competing theories of change popular in the literature, how do you know when to use a particular theory or technique? Does your favorite theory apply to all clients? If you see yourself as eclectic in theory usage, does this mean you lack knowledge of any theory in depth? Do you dismiss the eclectic model of theory-technique usage as too demanding for a graduate student? Has your pet theory been validated by research?

Chapter 6

FACILITATING CHANGE

How did you do in your efforts to change a problematic or habitual behavior problem? Did you try it? If not, how did you talk yourself out of this task? If you did the exercise, how long were you able to maintain the change? If you lapsed in your effort, did you resume your intention or give up? What beliefs about yourself did you discover in the inner chatter that accompanied your change efforts, either in relation to the decision to change or not to change or in the consequences of your decision? Do you intend to maintain the change beyond this point in time? If not, why not?

When students report back on the exercise requiring them to change a behavior pattern, there is usually considerable amusement as they hear of one another's struggles. The inner chatter aroused by struggles with change has by now lost its usual serious quality, and students observe more of the absurdity, exaggerations, and humor in their excuses and procrastination. A very important insight emerges from this discussion. The use of tasks with clients need not result in the solution to problems. Tasks are useful for at least two other reasons. First, they introduce the experience of choice quite directly. Tasks may be looked on as experiments wherein one can begin to play with one's own behavior rather than imagining oneself as solidly stuck in place. Even if one gives up a change effort after a day or two, one has shown that the change is a possibility. Students, like clients, will often modify a task from what was originally intended, because they find the modification more suitable.

One student's journal commentary stated:

> I chose to get up thirty minutes earlier each morning and to balance my checkbook. These are both pretty mundane activities, things that other people do with ease. After years of getting up at 5:30, sleep is sacred so this was difficult and wrought with much inner chatter. I succeeded three times to get up thirty minutes earlier, but now do not see it as something that will last. I wanted to find a time to meditate that wasn't full of "doing." I found I wasn't awake enough to meditate at that hour; better to stick with my tea. Even my cat worked against me in this effort to wake up. When he sensed that I was waking he would move to sit on my chest and purr as happy as he could, sort of saying, "You don't really want to do this." I believed him and stayed put. Out of this exercise I did find a time. Eleven at night comes to me as the perfect time and greatly enables my sleep. I found using baroque guitar music was a perfect friend in this new effort.

THEORETICAL ISSUES REGARDING CHANGE

Thus far we have concentrated your pursuit of practice wisdom upon the elements of subjectivity and religion/philosophical perspectives. While there have been occasional allusions to theory, we have not really engaged the complexities of integrating theory with subjectivity and religious/philosophical perspectives. It is one thing to note your personal struggles with problem change and your world design resistances to this. It is quite another matter to address the variations among clients as they deal with the frightening uncertainties of change.

When you reflected upon your own reactions to client resistances, perhaps you began to address the matter of integration of what you have learned about yourself with your use of theory. Remember that important piece of research regarding treatment effectiveness: No one theory proves itself superior to other theories in producing positive treatment outcomes. This was our point of departure for understanding the importance of practice wisdom. It is likely that the worker's personal integration of theory, subjectivity, and religious/philosophical perspectives is what accounts for positive treatment results, far more than the teachings of any given theory.

You will need to do your own personal integrating work in relation to theory or theories and what you have discovered about yourself as a person thus far. This is the nature of your ongoing process of practice wisdom development in the years ahead.

In the following pages I will share with you an eclectic model of treatment intervention that has made sense to me, and that I currently use with clients. It is not a model for your imitation, since it contains the prejudices, exclusions, and appealing interests that serve my personality, or world design. It may not fit you at all, even though it works for me.

In describing this interventive model, I will be using terms with which you are already familiar from the preceding chapters. The key terms are *world design, situation,* and *awareness.* I will reference for you those treatment theories I have found most applicable as we proceed through a study of the model. Perhaps the most important learning for you, in this model, is to see a consistency of thinking that integrates previous discussions of subjectivity and philosophical perspectives with theory differences. Bear in mind that your own integration efforts with theory may be quite different from, even opposite to, those I share with you. That is all for the good. We are different people and our profession is still in the throes of theory-practice development. While research on psychotherapy and social work treatment seems to underscore the management of the therapeutic relationship as most important, students in graduate schools have a different priority. Out of their fear of an array of potentially troubled clients, many of whom represent strange and foreign life-styles and attitudes, students want theory that will reassure them. They hope theory will explain the oddities that confront them and assure them about what they can or cannot hope to accomplish. Being pragmatic Americans, by and large, students also bring their belief in progress through technology to their expectations of graduate learning. They want to learn techniques that will help clients out of the maze and mire of their problematic lives. These two hopes, of a true theory and of effective techniques, do more to misguide students from practice wisdom than any other aspect of their graduate education.

On the other hand, it is far too nebulous to speak of "unique world designs" and the "use of self, therapeutically." While these are both key concepts in the subject of practice wisdom, they can be appreciated only as brief glimpses of truth. They become valid, integrated experiences after students have exposed themselves to both theoretical formulations and an arsenal of skills or techniques.

A useful point of departure is the differentiation between client centeredness and theory centeredness. Client centeredness is a perspective that can be related to diagnosis, prognosis, goal setting, theme detection (in interviews), and discovering the solutions to problems (Krill, 1978, chaps. 8, 9).

```
Client Centeredness
      diagnosis
      prognosis
      goal setting
    theme detection
    problem solution
```

While this is somewhat oversimplified, the main point is that the client is our central point for knowledge rather than a theory we may be tempted to use as an explanation of and recipe for the client.

- *Diagnosis:* Each person is his or her own diagnostic category. It is far more important to understand what is special about the client than what is generalizable.
- *Prognosis:* Clients are credited with the ability to change in whatever ways they believe themselves capable of changing. They may in time prove themselves wrong, but at least they are not being reinforced by pessimistic worker conclusions.
- *Goal setting:* Clients vary in their views of how change occurs and what type of changes seem needed, and these unique perspectives need to be appreciated. Diagnosis, as clinical category, should not determine goals.
- *Theme detection:* Each interview reveals a theme of primary concern arising from the client. This will not always be obvious, but it must be discovered and revealed if therapeutic engagement is to occur. It is presumptuous and mechanistic for the worker to set the theme on the basis of what he or she thinks a client needs.
- *Problem solution:* Clients have the solutions to their problems available to them, but are failing to heed or access them. Solutions are found in memory, in here-and-now awareness, and with the help of family members and friends who know the clients well.

```
A:  awareness (unknown)
WD: world design (known)
S:  situation (given)

Solutions and Clarity
        past
      present
       future
       others
```

The three concepts of awareness, world design, and situation will be used to illustrate variations in the process of technique intervention. *Awareness* refers to the unknowns of one's here-and-now experience. While this present experiencing appears to be made up of what is already known, this is a falsification of thinking used to reassure oneself about one's stable world design. In fact, the here-and-now moment of awareness is beyond what we already know from our past. We are always in a process of change, as are our surroundings, so even though there will be similarities, each moment is pregnant with unknown potential for personal integration in response to the given elements of our situation. *World design*, on the other hand, is known (or at least accessible) because it is derived from memory. The *situation* is a given that we may or may not have predicted and influenced. It may be experienced as absurd and unwanted or it may be experienced as personal destiny. In either case, it is what is happening, what is offered, what is there.

Counseling is a process of problem clarification and problem solving. Clarifications or solutions are rooted in the client's experience of past, present, and future, and in his or her relationships with others.

Past memories are a treasure chest of usable information for the client. When the worker enables the client to discover his or her own potential clarity for problem solution, the worker sidesteps the problem of generating resistance. Resistance commonly results from the client's effort to maintain some sense of autonomy when confronted by advice from the counselor. The storehouse of client knowledge begins with interest in what the client has tried to do about the problem and how the client understands the nature of the problem. But knowledge interest is quickly expanded. What similar problems did the client have in the past, why, and how were they dealt with? What have others said about the problem and what might be done about it? How did the client's family members handle such problems when the client was a child? If this did not occur as a problem challenge in the client's immediate family, what about his or her relatives and friends, or his or her spouse's relatives and friends? How did they handle such problems? What has the client learned from reading and watching television and movies about how people handle such problems? At times when the client's life seems momentarily free of this problem (vacation? when specific people visit? a couple of "good days" for no apparent reason?), what is different for him or her?

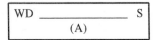

WD _____ S
(A)

What the worker is attempting in this pursuit of the past is to help the client access his or her own world design in detail, as the client's memories may be relevant to the present problematic situation. There is no effort made to heighten here-and-now awareness, as this is not necessary at this point. The above diagram illustrates this emphasis.

Present experiencing is another source of clarity and problem solution discovery. Here the problem is not so much the failure to access available knowledge, but inner conflict related to change. This conflict may be related to unfinished business that splits our energy and interest. One feels that one cannot make a single-minded effort for change when there appear to be troubling and major issues still unsatisfactorily dealt with and therefore incomplete. Yet one is required to address a new issue whether one feels prepared or not.

One method of handling such a dilemma is to recognize, accept, and shelve unfinished business and intentionally give a wholehearted effort to the task at hand. One utilizes one's creative response, one's attention to "what needs doing," and gets on with it. Unfinished business is left for another time, another day, or to somehow resolve itself. Here the therapeutic methods of Milton Erickson, Roberto Assagioli (1965), and David Reynolds (1984) are applicable. Diagrammatically, this intervention would appear like this:

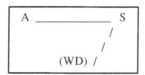

One is primarily utilizing one's here-and-now awareness in order to discover an attentive and possibly creative response to the situation. World design is involved, but not centrally. World design is clearly related to the responsibilities one has already established in one's life, to the knowledge one has about many of the elements in one's situation, and to an assessment of ways one might respond in this situation. One might say that world design is involved in its pragmatic sense, but not in its protective, security-conscious sense.

A very different way to handle unfinished business is to conduct an exploration of the conflict itself. The conflict is exaggerated, intensified, given total attention. Opposing sides to the conflict are developed and identified with. Fears that interfere with resolution of the problem are explored. The risk of such efforts is that therapy may promote a self-centered intellectualization or repetitive emotion about the conflict. In order to avoid this, the worker should seek to promote humor, self-disgust, anger, and choosing. The therapeutic methods of Gestalt therapy (Perls, 1969), cognitive therapy (Ellis, 1974), provocative therapy (Farrelly, 1974), and aspects of psychoanalytic ego psychology (Strean, 1979) can be used effectively for these purposes. Diagrammatically, this intervention appears like this:

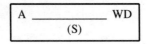

The process of work is between the client's world design of fixed ideas and his or her awareness as a source of new insight or revelation. The situation is put on hold until the client has a clear sense of what he or she wants to do in relation to it. It is generally a mistake to use this intervention over a prolonged period of time, but it is an effective and powerful method when used with discrimination and when choosing is emphasized.

Future direction and/or a sense of personal commitment is another useful source for problem clarity and solutions. One way to understand the client's future is to see what may be potentially realizable in his or her immediately coming life. Here the use of dream work and guided fantasy may be helpful, enabling the client to generate some of the integrative messages from his or her heart, or subconscious, as to potential new directions opening up for consideration. This is another expression of the diagram used above in which the focus is upon the client's own dialogue between awareness and world design, as the client sees potential modification in his or her world design. The writings in Gestalt and psychosynthesis, aforementioned, are applicable here.

The other method used to address future direction is that suggested by Victor Frankl (1965) and Irwin Yalom (1980), where the problem is experienced as a lack of personal meaning, direction, or destiny. One helps the client to look at previous sources of meaningful satisfaction in his or her life and the opportunities for reaffirming some of this within future plans. This may also involve further exploration into the client's religious or philosophical orientations and what these have to say to him or her now. Do these beliefs require clarification or new directions, or does the client need to be considering a new quest for life understanding? Here the diagram might appear like that used in assessing past memories in relation to the client's current situation, with world design and situation as the primary focus of counseling.

Others who are significant in the client's life need to be involved directly or indirectly in the treatment when the problem centers upon a breakdown, loss, or sense of alienation, continuing conflict, or mutual isolation in important relationships. Again, the source of clarity and problem solution is found by the client within his or her own existing system of relationships, or within him- or herself as he or she sees the lack of relationships and the powerful need for them. Family therapy models (Nichols, 1984) are especially useful here, as the focus is upon the client's issues of intimacy; mutual and stable respect, support, and appreciation; working out of unresolved conflicts; and seeking to establish new relationships. Diagrammatically we could look upon these efforts in this way:

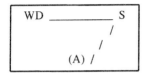

This diagram would apply not only to the client, but to others involved in the therapy process. Focus is upon world designs of individuals interacting with the significant others of the situation. Occasionally, here-and-now awareness may be used as a means of helping people define for themselves some of the new and emerging aspects of themselves that need to be addressed interpersonally. This is of central importance when the primary goal is enhancing intimacy by lessening the manipulative and stereotypical patterns in the relationship.

Relationship issues with others must occasionally begin by focusing upon the client's mode of relating to the worker. So transference-countertransference interpretations can be a useful means of helping the client take a step toward work with significant others. A useful safeguard, however, is for the worker to appreciate that the client's relationships with others are of far more importance than the client's relationship with the worker. Therapy is not concluded with the client's realization of the transference issues he or she has with the worker. Therapy with significant others is now ready to begin. In addressing transference issues it is generally a mistake to focus upon historical and traumatic memories over a long period so as to "work them through." Rather, the client needs to come quickly to appreciate those aspects of his or her world design that interfere with current relationships. The choice is then between experimenting with new modes of transference-free behavior and working directly with members of the family of origin so as to resolve painful unfinished business in that system. Again we find that the source of clarity and problem solution can be found within the client and the others of significance in his or her life. The client is helped to clarify his or her existing world design conclusions and how these impede relationships now. The client is further aided in assessing what it is he or she wants in relation to other people.

It should be clear from the above illustration that certain theories and methods are either left out or minimally used. Both behavior modification and psychoanalytic ego psychology are of limited value here. The reason for this is that both of these models tend to disempower the client by placing the expertise of either task design or theoretical interpretations in the hands of the worker. It is true that both of these models may be used effectively by a worker possessing practice wisdom. They can sensitively find both task ideas and insights within the client, but, because of the ways in which these methods are too often practiced, this is the exception rather than the rule.

Even the cognitive, problem-solving, and strategic models of treatment popular now in graduate training run the risk of disempowering clients or limiting the worker's appreciation of the client's world design. Limiting the helping role to the efficiency of symptom relief fails to appreciate the existential dilemmas behind so many clients' problems. If a problem is a natural expression of a person's world design, rather than a foreign intruder, then world design issues need to be somehow addressed. The notion that the client will seek help again, if needed beyond the symptom relief, is simply another version of terminating treatment when transference issues with the worker are understood and resolved. The dual-focus model of social work addresses both world design and life situation. Problems are an invitation to the client for an important understanding as to what it means for him or her to be a human being within the circumstances of a given life situation. We are not mere technicians, but also facilitators of human learning.

So there you have my model, biases and all. If you found yourself reacting negatively to portions of it, you have some important clues as to your own preferences and a direction for your personal integration of theory with who you are.

Having surveyed the many variations on how one might facilitate client change, you should be left with an important question: How does the worker know when to use a particular intervention with a given client? This is the very point of doubt (and anxiety) that drives many students back to a theory-centered model. They hope that their clinical diagnoses will inform them as to the methods required. There is another alternative, which I have found far more preferable. The relationship between you and the client can existentially direct you to the appropriate intervention. This will be the subject of the next chapter. In preparation for Chapter 7, and as a follow-up to your inner chatter study from Chapter 5, we need first to address the implications of that exercise.

INNER CHATTER AND BEYOND

The inner chatter study was a refinement for your own awareness of just how subtle and comprehensive the rule of your inner chatter is. If you did this exercise you may have been alarmed by the tyrannical power of your own world design. Remind yourself that your world design and its defensive chatter is your natural way of survival. Appreciate your need for an individual identity. Yet your alarm is also quite appropriate, because world design allegiance does impair both creativity and intimacy.

How do we transcend our world design? It is useful to reflect upon different ways of knowing:

> *Forms of Knowing*
>
> nonthinking
> thought as labeling
> conceptualizing

We may know something apart from any active thought process, as often occurs with intuition or simple habitual behaviors such as in driving a car through traffic. There is usually an immediacy of response in such intuitive knowing. This also occurs in the helping process when we respond spontaneously to a client.

We may also attach words as labels for our experience. Here we are activating our memory process as a means of identifying what we are experiencing, yet we are not conceptualizing or evaluating the experience. We commonly do this when we are in a state of empathy with a client and are called upon to interact with words at the same time.

The third form of thinking, conceptualizing, is what characterizes our inner chatter. We pursue cause-effect speculations, analysis, conclusions, worry, regrets, and so on. While there is a valid place for such reasoned thinking, we too often use it when there is no need to do so. The result is an imposition of our thoughts upon an experience, which can have the negative effect of narrowing, rigidifying, or stereotyping an experience and even of alienating ourselves from what is actually occurring before us.

A meditative practice for seeing how these forms of knowing arise is as follows. While traveling alone, whether by car, bike, or public transport, note your inner chatter. Now attend to what you see outside as you move along and see what thoughts are triggered in you. Next, simply label (in any way) varied visual observations, such as "passing-passing," as you pass other vehicles, "slowing-slowing," as you slow down, "clouding-clouding," as you see clouds, "signing-signing," as you note signs. Finally, let yourself stay with this series of simple observations, but without words, allowing inner silence.

A similar exercise can be applied to one's personal awareness of inner emotions at any time, as recommended by Krishnamurti (1968, p. 63). Instead of the usual response to troubled feelings (I am angry because . . . , or I am fearful because . . .), simply label the emotive state as "angering-angering" or "fearing-fearing." You may disregard the speculations and evaluations (especially when they are doing no good anyway, other than draining energy and intensifying the troubled emotion). This also avoids needless partializing of your own experience. One simply accepts the subjective process as a happening process.

In preparation for the next chapter it will be important to sensitize yourself as to how you avoid personal intimacy in relationships. You can do this exercise while engaging clients, or with your friends and peers.

Attending to intimacy avoidance. Attend to the interactive processes between you and others; note how you avoid intimacy. There are times when such avoidance may be not only appropriate but desirable. Do you also find yourself sometimes avoiding intimacy even at moments when you desire it? Do you allow intimacy with clients?

> *Intimacy Avoidance*
>
> domination/submission
> manipulation
> indifferent observer
> detached witness
> fusion
> decoupling

These examples of avoidance are provided as a guide for you to evaluate your own deceptions, manipulations, and planned strategies for sidestepping intimacy (Offman, 1976). The examples are defined as follows:

- *domination/submission:* relating to another person as if you are superior/inferior to the other
- *manipulation:* relating to another as if he or she were an object for your use in accomplishing some desired task or goal

- *indifferent observer:* imagining that you are not a part of a relationship with another person as you analyze and objectify him or her
- *detached witness:* seeking one-sided openness in a relationship by providing no reciprocity or honest feedback to the other as to how you are being affected by the relationship
- *fusion:* failing to differentiate your personal response to another; losing your sense of self in empathy so as to not be detached, yet avoiding individuation of self
- *decoupling:* withdrawing from a personal response being sought by another (includes silence, changing the subject, joking, provocative yet deflective comments, and mystification—interpreting the other's statement as not really applicable to you, as is sometimes done with transference)

Chapter 7

PROFESSIONAL INTENSITY

How did you respond to the previous chapter? Were you bored or intellectually stimulated by the ideas? Did you imagine the ideas were too complex and beyond you, or that the model was an oversimplification of theory and method? Did you think that the content was simply intellectual and missed the heart of the therapeutic process?

Depending upon your primary mode of learning (cognitive, intuitive, emotional, sensual), your responses are probably quite different from those of students who utilize a primary mode that is different from the one you prefer. Your level of intelligence, previous experiences with clients, readings/supervision/classroom experiences, and emotional mood at the time you read the chapter might also be important forces determining your reaction. These same variations operate in our clients, of course, and this is one important reason our interventions are sometimes effective and other times not.

When I teach the material and exercises you have been following, I find that by this time students in class are reporting changes and surprises in their work with clients. While they tend to attribute these changes to the personal effects of this course, there are numerous other experiences affecting them at the same time, from their fieldwork, their other classes, and their personal lives.

There is a lessening of a need to rescue, or even to "do something" in response to client bids for help. The students often feel a greater intensity with their clients in terms of empathy and in allowing themselves to be more free or spontaneous. Diagnosis and theory complexities no longer seem so threatening to their personal self-esteem. They often find themselves more personal with their supervisors, and are pleasantly surprised at their supervisors' positive responses to them. The therapy process has become far less mysterious and much more human.

The basic message to be set forth in this chapter is that who you are is far more important for successful and satisfying interventions with clients than what you know. Theory supplements self-understanding in useful ways, but it is not the primary factor on the road to practice wisdom.

There is an intensity possible within the worker-client relationship that is too often lacking in the content of our readings. It is sometimes experienced when we have the privilege of observing a master counselor in action by means of one-way mirror, videotape, or live demonstration. We can even gain a glimmer of this intensity in occasional readings that provide verbatim interview exchanges. An excellent book that reveals this kind of occurrence is Corsini, Standal, and Stanelly's *Critical Incidents in Psychotherapy* (1959), a collection of vignettes by novice counselors that produced profound turnabouts with their clients. The commentaries on the chapters by various theoreticians are almost humorous because of their explanations of why the changes occurred. The commentaries are not only varied, they are often in opposition to what others are saying.

Among psychotherapists who successfully convey consistent interview intensity are William Offman, Walter Kempler, Carl Rogers, Frank Farrelly, and Anna Cohlm. While one can occasionally find examples of such intensity in the writings of many authors, these particular counselors emphasize such intensity as the heart of their therapeutic work.

The intensity of the worker-client relationship seems to wax and wane. We sometimes anticipate that intensity will occur with a client, and it does not. Other times we are tired or expect another dull session with a tiresome client and are pleasantly surprised with the intense connection that arises. We shall be exploring this elusive element of the counseling process, with the idea that this may be the most important feature of effective therapeutic work. We hope to discover clues herein as to why workers select specific interventions with particular clients.

There is a role-play exercise I do in my classes that I recommend you do with your working partner, or with any student peer who is willing to cooperate. I share this exercise early in this chapter because I would like you to be reflecting upon its possibilities for your own learning as you read the rest of the chapter.

Doing "poor therapy" in role play. Students are instructed to pair off and to take turns role-playing a client and a worker interviewing the client. Prior to the first role play, the teacher meets with the interviewers while students who will be "clients" are outside the room thinking up their particular role plays. The interviewers are given these instructions:

> Allow yourself to interview in a style different from your usual style. Let yourself do "poor therapy," if such is the case. Permit yourself to play with the client as well as with your own spontaneity. Have no worry about the results. If you want to be somewhat outrageous, let it happen. The role play will be limited to 15 minutes.

After the first role play, and before any discussion or feedback, the roles are reversed and the teacher instructs the new interviewers in the same fashion. After the second role play, students give one another feedback about both role plays; this is followed by discussion among the entire class.

The subsequent feedback to this exercise is remarkable. As might be expected, the "poor therapy" turns out, in most cases, to be exceedingly "good and effective therapy." Spontaneity, playfulness, and intensity are brought to a higher pitch than ever before. Students see that their own inhibitions, cautions, and fears may actually be impeding their use of self from more directly human and productive ways of being with a client.

Now let us turn to the intimacy avoidance exercise you did in preparation for the reading of this chapter. The issue, of course, was not whether or not you avoid intimacy, but rather *how* you avoid it. It is foolish not to avoid intimacy under many occasions. We lack the energy, trust, and potential for reciprocity in a goodly number of our social exchanges. Some would say there is even a real danger to intimacy whenever it occurs. They would pose this characteristic of the human condition: The more two people seek intimacy, the more likely they are to encounter conflict, a lack of interest, or a failure to understand one another.

Here is an example of a journal response of a student to the exercise on intimacy avoidance. Some students did the exercise with their dyad partners who shared in the course.

> When I have an expectation of the outcome, or want something from the other, dialogue is interfered with. Another common problem is the lack of a common language, which is based on experience and one's personal history of use of the words employed, and one's personal history with the meaning of the perceived nonverbal communication occurring. This be-

came readily apparent in my listening to my class "partner," and my realization that I was continually "scanning" my own experience to try to understand what he was saying. Similarly, listening to my own inner chatter, as well as the "spinning out" with my own thoughts, and the "waiting" to say what I want to say, all got in the way of dialogue. Sharing this with my partner brought concurrence from him . . . he was experiencing the same thing. In dialogue with my partner I know it is essential to be open and straight and feel I can do that well, at least with someone who seems to respond, and who also seems amazingly like me in thoughts and feelings. It's a tremendous mystery to me how he and I "found" each other, never having met before, and managed to be two people so alike. I've puzzled over whether or not I can respond as well to those who seem, at least on the surface, totally "alien" to my way of thinking. Then I get caught up in the question of which came first, our "alikeness" or our willingness to be genuine with each other, which might be *transcending* any apparent differences!

PROFESSIONAL INTENSITY AND USE OF SELF

There is a difference between intimacy and professional intensity. Intimacy could be considered one form, among others, of professional intensity. Intimacy may or may not be useful with a specific client. Professional intensity is always desirable, not only for the client but also for the worker's well-being. As noted in the previous chapter, a worker may sometimes deliberately discourage intimacy between him- or herself and the client because the more important task is that of generating intimacy between the client and other family members. Yet this very effort to facilitate family intimacy, or even to know when it is appropriate to do so, calls for the use of professional intensity.

Professional intensity takes three interrelated forms: detached caring, techniques as creative emergence, and managing motivations. Each is described in turn below.

DETACHED CARING

In your role as counselor, when do you find yourself most enjoying an interview with a client? What is happening within yourself? How does this contrast to those interviews you do not enjoy, and perhaps sometimes dread? If you reflect on these questions, you will quickly note that enjoyable interviews are either free of, or move beyond, experiences of boredom, anxiety, irritation, seductive fantasies, suspicion, anger, and idle thoughts unrelated to the client. Your passion is aroused in genuine client interest and concern. At times of shared, unrelenting pain, you may be more apt to describe your interview response as "vitally connected" than enjoyable. Caring with passion (compassion) is an essential ingredient of satisfactory counseling.

On the other hand, you may have found that despite your compassion, the client does not return again, or does not really seem to have changed for the better. This worries you and you wonder, Have I overidentified with this client? If you have, you might say that what felt to you like compassion was self-pity in disguise. Another version of this self-pity is vengeance. You want to get at some "persecutor" through your client "victim." Still a third rendition of overidentifying self-pity is the desire to rescue the client so he or she will stop hurting, because it is adding to your own pain. These are examples of what is also referred to as countertransference. To guard against this phenomenon requires some level of detachment—that is, a clear differentiation of your own sense of self from that of the client. One may "feel with" but not "become one with." This is the difference between compassion and fusion.

Two earlier exercises offered you the possibility of detached caring: being with a client without thinking and experiencing a client's pain as the perfect place to be. Both of these exercises encourage the differentiation of oneself by limiting one's own world design concerns so as to appreciate better the person of the client.

TECHNIQUES AS CREATIVE EMERGENCE

There is a second characteristic to a deeply satisfying interview: the sense of sufficiency. This occurs when your activity in a session fits well with the needs of the client at that particular time. Another counselor may act quite differently from you, yet manage an equally effective fit. How is this possible? In an interview with an individual client, there are two people involved. Both have the possibility of engaging their own creative processes. Your personal creative process reflects your unique integration of professional knowledge with yourself as a person today—at this specific point in your life. Your integration of these two factors is also responding to what your client is presenting of him- or herself to you at this time. Like a dawning gestalt, an emerging understanding, a revealing sense of certainty, one knows what to do and does it. The combination of empathy and reflective thought usually accompanies such an experience. We may sometimes refer to this happening as intuitive, or a hunch, but we are actually drawing upon some reservoir of integrated understanding within ourselves. Martin Buber would prefer to describe this occurrence as knowledge being revealed *between* oneself and one's client, as he speaks of the I-thou experience of dialogue (Friedman, 1960, chap. 14).

Students reporting pleasant surprise with their role play of doing poor therapy are often reporting upon this very spontaneous happening. They have, for the moment, freed themselves from what they imagine to be a supervisor's expectations, or from some mental construction based in reading or class as to what is "good therapy." They have allowed something special about their personal responses in the interview to be revealed. This is not to say that theory has not been a help, but it is not the strict determinant of their actions.

MANAGING MOTIVATIONS

A third characteristic of interview satisfaction is aliveness. Vitality can be contagious. If the client is lacking in aliveness, because of the deadening effects of his or her self-preoccupations and repetitive frustrating conclusions, the worker has a clear-cut task: to stimulate hope or problem engagement on the part of the client. How often have you felt dragged into the quagmire of the client's mood? You find yourself glancing at the time, looking forward to the end of the session. You may have been adequately empathic, but you find no emerging sense of what to do. The efforts you have made have felt somewhat mechanical and have not produced the slightest dent in the client's protective armor. Your own inner chatter mounts for a while, as you wonder what is going on, what to do, then it may shift to personal fantasies that have nothing to do with the client. Catching yourself, you feel a bit chagrined and return to empathy. But now the empathy produces nothing more than weariness, and you fight back a yawn. You will have to think this one through later, perhaps with your supervisor. Or you may reassure yourself that you are really doing an adequate job; that what the client needs is a listening ear and nothing more. In time the client will feel accepted and properly nurtured and will then be open for some more exciting change efforts. But in subsequent sessions your resentment grows, for the client does not respond to your martyrlike patience. Instead of generating a "contact high" for the client, the client has generated a "contact low" in you!

In addressing this sort of problem it can be reassuring to remind yourself that while nothing useful may be happening with a client, this is not necessarily your fault. One cannot impose vitality, only offer it. If it is refused, and one sees no alternative ways of enlivening the process, it is often best to resort to honesty. The disturbance of honesty is usually preferable to the nonverbal dishonesty that implies "we are having a useful session" when in reality you are both contributing to each other's sense of alienation and dullness. Honesty might take the form of outward yawning, deliberate checking of the time, falling asleep, suggesting that the session be terminated early, inquiring what the client thinks or feels is being accomplished, sharing your own sense of dullness with the proceedings, pressing for some decision as to what the client intends to do about his or her jumbled complaints, or the like.

As a student, you may not feel all that secure with some of the above negative expressions (What will my supervisor say?!). It is certainly preferable for you to incite spontaneity and alertness in your client before the interview grinds to such a point of unresponsive lethargy. But how does one do this—especially if you dutifully "start where the client is"?

How do you show vitality with your friends when you are feeling good? How are you spontaneous with children and animals? A psychotherapist once described his therapeutic model to me as doing play therapy with adults. Frank Farrelly (1974) points out that most of us have emotive comments about even our dullest clients when gossiping about them with peers or spouses. He recommends taking "coffee-room" talk into the session with the client to see how you can make constructive use of your emotional responses. Farrelly illustrates how the use of humor and the provocation of anger and self-disgust in clients is a healing force for both client and worker. Whittaker (in Neil & Kriskern, 1982), Kempler (1973), and Offman (1976) are quite open with clients about their own personal need for enjoyment or vitality. They are equally clear that this is a two-way process and it is up to the client or family to participate by engaging the therapist through their own emotions. Counseling for these master therapists seems almost like a battleground at times.

"But I'm only a student," you will protest. "Those guys have years of experience!" True, but remember there are many, many counselors with years of experience who have become rigid or burned-out zombies. Others fled into administrative, research, or teaching positions. If you are going to humanize your work with clients, you had better begin now. Stop imitating other counselors or living out your theoretical expectations of what you should ideally be. Deal with yourself as a person reacting in concrete circumstances with clients. Tape interviews and let yourself respond critically to what you hear. At what points are you embarrassed or annoyed with your performance? Can you detect dullness, insecurity, phoniness in your own voice? What about those good moments of laughter and intensity—how could you expand them?

The intimacy avoidance exercise discussed earlier in this chapter is an excellent indicator of how you may be sidestepping opportunities for spontaneity and emotional engagement with others. Since this is the work of your precious world design, chances are you disrupt or fail to attend to vitality possibilities with clients in similar ways. The sensitivity or encounter groups popular in the early 1970s were laboratory experiments for detecting intimacy avoidance. As the student journal response to the intimacy exercise above shows, it is quite possible for even a student dyad to explore together the comings and goings of vitality and honesty. Student self-help groups are sometimes devised for this same purpose. Release and spontaneous expression are necessary; self-knowledge and insights are not enough. Self-help groups for student helpers can include sharing of tapes to reveal student interchanges with clients. This helps focus group discussions on areas that are immediately relevant, as opposed to spinning wheels over one another's past traumas.

ASSIGNMENTS

The next chapter will focus upon matters of spirituality and attitudes toward institutionalized religion. In preparation for this discussion, there are two exercises you need to accomplish before moving into Chapter 8.

Reactions to institutionalized religions. What does institutionalized religion mean to you? What emotional reactions surface for you about this topic? What personal experiences come to mind as likely origins for your reactions? Knowing that the majority of economically deprived and minority clients are members of churches, what steps have you taken to address your personal biases about religion?

Archetype exploration. You will recall our discussion of archetypes in Chapter 1. Archetype images reveal existing potentials within ourselves that can sometimes provide us a sense of hope, inspiration, and personal direction. We may or may not have activated these possibilities. It can be most useful for your own growth and freedom from your habitual world design to know some of the characteristics that compose your favored archetypes. You can even compose an image of yourself that incorporates some of these characteristics. Your task is to construct one or more personal archetype images and describe the characteristics of these. Since archetype images are said to stem from our integrative-creative unconscious, they are often outside our ordinary awareness.

While they most commonly appear in dreams and daydreams, they can also be sensed through specific forms to which we find ourselves intensely attracted. As a means of exploring such attractions, you are asked to reflect on each of the forms listed in the following box.

```
            Archetype Potentials

         (1)  animal
         (2)  force in nature
         (3)  hero-heroine models
         (4)  human-made object
         (5)  symbol
```

You may wish to review the hero-heroine models exercise done in Chapter 1 and see how the characteristics you pinpointed may tie in with the other forms being explored.

You will be considering a force in nature of special appeal (e.g., tree, storm, sea, mountain); a favorite bird, animal, fish, or reptile; a prized human-made object (perhaps found on your desk or mantle at home); and a symbol of special, positive meaning for you. Combine these with your hero-heroine characteristics and be prepared to use this image in the next chapter.

Chapter 8

MATTERS OF SPIRITUALITY

C. G. Jung spoke of archetypes as power forces that dwell within our unconscious and that can be utilized for growth or individuation (Schaer, 1950). These forces are both within us and beyond us, shared by our culture, some shared by all of humanity. Religious symbols enable many people to connect personally with their own archetype images. Such images can also be identified through our dreams and artistic expressions. As indicated in the Chapter 7, you may have clues to some of your archetype images as a result of certain preferences for and attractions to forces in nature, special people, symbols, and so on. How did you do with the task of conceptualizing an image of yourself by integrating your archetype images?

Students are often confused about how to link archetype images with their own self-identities so as to see them as realistic personal potentials. Here are some examples from student journals.

It's interesting for me to look at the things that I have chosen to help me name my archetype . . . the ocean, a racehorse, pottery wind chimes, and a star. The ocean because it is vast and powerful, and always moving. Always moving, whether it is calm and gently rolling, or angry and thrashing. A racehorse because it is powerful, graceful, spirited, gentle, willful, and strong . . . and it knows what it is running toward and it moves toward that mark. . . . Often it wears blinders so that it will not be distracted by things that do not matter. I like that. Wind chimes of a potter. Pottery because it is made from the earth, as am I. So in a sense "pottery" and I are both "one" with nature. Wind chimes because they catch the wind and create from it, while it blows, a song that is beautiful. A star for several reasons, I suppose. I love to look at them . . . they are mysterious and light the darkness of the night. Once I found one in a box during a guided meditation . . . it was a special gift to me. Maybe that represented a bit of grandiosity, but I think that more than that it represents an effortless presence . . . a being. The stars shine for all to see. They are hidden by nothing. And they are, they simply are. And so the archetype that I see in myself through all of this is that of a gentle warrior and an explorer. One who is looking and pressing forward, and moving toward "the mark." Yet one whose "battles" are gentle . . . one who is connected to the miracles of the universe, one who moves, sometimes gently and sometimes very deliberately, but always with great force. One who is gentle, too. Mostly, one who simply is.

There are basically three archetypes that I could identify that I see somewhat in myself and can relate to as typical models. According to my needs and what's going on in my life, different archetypes are more predominant than the others at different given times. One that I could identify with is similar to "Mother Earth." I prefer to think of it as a personified "Indian woman" (no particular tribe, though I am thinking Native American). This conjures up images of nature, appreciating natural beauty, grace, caring, and nurturing. There is also the idea of being at peace, the calm, gentle, naturally wise sense of self. Another archetype that frequently saves my sanity is the "court jester." This is the character that doesn't make fun of, but makes light of life and its pressures and stresses. What's the worst that can happen? This person in me helps me put life's situations in perspective. The third archetype is the loyal, dependable worker. This applies to academic, practice, and life's task work. "Ya gotta do what'cha gotta do," whether for basic survival or to succeed in an endeavor.

I recognize and try to maintain contact with four inner figures: a wise old man/guide, a woman, a fool, an outlaw. The wise old man appears, sometimes, in the form of a Zen masterlike man, sometimes as a gray-bearded "ancient" who points the way for me, and sometimes as a Tibetan nomad (who travels, with his family, on the vast steppes of Asia, visiting towns occasionally to visit with the people of magic and wisdom in the town). The principal characteristics of "the woman" are a wild humor, sensuality, and loving and nurturing intuition. The "fool" has been alluded to throughout the journal (the visual image I use is the Tarot fool in the Tarot deck) and is the principal ally at this time in my life. The "outlaw" comes and goes (of course, he's an outlaw) but reminds me to avoid identification with the "goodies" of the law (society and culture) in favor of independence to seek my own life's expression.

Do these ideas help you? Let's try two short exercises with your imagination. You will be using an image of yourself based upon one or more of the characteristics of your archetypes.

Close your eyes and relax. Imagine yourself emulating one or more of the archetype images you have specified. In order to do this you need to imagine yourself in a situation that calls for the use of this characteristic. If you meet with a strange inner resistance to continuing the exercise, you should give full attention to the resistance and not proceed unless the resistance disappears. This exercise lasts about 3 minutes.

The second exercise focuses upon problem solving. Reflect upon a current problem in your life that you would like to have changed. It is a problem that you can see you have a part in maintaining. With eyes closed, you are to imagine yourself as incorporating one or more of your archetype images and to see how you deal with the problem under the circumstances of your problem situation. You may spend up to 5 minutes with this exercise.

The purpose of this exercise is to illustrate how problems can sometimes be handled effectively by tapping into the creative aspects of personality rather than seeking cause-effect explanations or even practical and reasoned-out tasks for change. This way of thinking is compatible with the writings of Roberto Assagioli (1965). This exercise is an example of a technique that deals with the interplay between *world design* and *awareness*, apart from any actual situation, as discussed in Chapter 6.

Some would refer to the source of archetypes as our spiritual nature, because they seem to exist autonomously, apart from our self-created world design. Jung specified the Self as different from the self, emphasizing the former to be our Soul while the latter is our persona and shadow.

As we begin to explore ideas about spirituality and religion, I would like you to do an exercise. Figure 8.1 provides four labeled quadrants. This exercise asks you to reflect upon your concept of G___. You may fill in the blank as you wish. Some might say God, Goddess, Godot, godlessness. You may write directly on the figure or transfer the quadrants to your journal. Jot down capsule statements that answer these four inquiries:

Your concept of G___ when you were a child.
Your concept of G___ now.
A view of G___ you wish you had, but don't.
Your response to views of G___ that differ from your own.

You should take from 5 to 10 minutes to complete this exercise.

You have been asked to reflect upon your attitudes about institutionalized religion. Are the attitudes you developed consistent with the

when you were a child	now

wished for	response to differing views

Figure 8.1 Concept of G___

exercise on G___ that you just completed? If not, what are the points of discrepancy? The following comments related to religion are from student journals.

> I have a real problem with some religious adherents whom I see as dogmatic, judgmental, and salvation-excluding, especially those convinced of their teachings of absolute infallibility, and those who prey on the guilt and innocence of others. I draw a distinction between religions and religious believers, and if the interpretation of a religion creates a dysfunction in a client's life, I will try to help the client take a different view of that belief.

> I was nervous to tell her my religious stance, for I thought she would disagree. It would have been fine if she had, but actually we both share the same belief about religion. We were both quite surprised. I feel that people are threatened by you if you don't believe in God. We both feel strongly that religion has caused a lot of human kinds of misery. Look at how the Catholics make their children feel about sex. We both were inspired by our conversation and felt good about the way we believe. I know that I feel positive about my beliefs. Also, it does not infringe upon us for others to believe the way they do. I run into people all the time who strongly believe in God and religion, and I am less willing to share my beliefs, but I accept theirs.

> Religion is a hard concept for me to get a fix on. Spirituality is wonderful for me . . . it is a discovery and an opening of doors. Yet organized "religion" is an ambivalent idea for me. It can be a way to organize beliefs, yet when that happens it sometimes grows into a set of rigid rules instead of a series of beliefs that are "in process." I think that Woody Allen was right when he said, "If Jesus were to come back today, He'd never stop throwing up at some of the things being done in His name." Organized religion hurts and excludes people with its "rules," yet it shouldn't. It should invite people to discover and explore the fullness of who they are. But since it doesn't (at least not according to my experience), I prefer "spirituality" to "religion." Spirituality is the essence of what I believe life to be and how I perceive the mysteries and miracles of life. It may be different for everyone . . . yet I think that it is recognizing the truths that are beyond us as individuals. In my mind, "religion" becomes perverse when it becomes a list of rules imposed by a group of people who are "religious." I think that when this occurs the essence of the truth is lost or, worse yet, it is twisted into something that it is not. For me there are certain basics which are one foundation of my "religious" beliefs . . . and they are vital. How I build on that foundation has surely changed over the years and will continue to change, yet "the foundation" pretty much remains the same.

After the death of my father, I *became atheist* partly due to my inability
to go to temple daily and praise God for "His" greatness after taking my
father in such an inhumane manner. Then many months later, I read a book
called *When Bad Things Happen to Good People*. In this book the author
explains his theory that God is not all-powerful and that there exists a
randomness in the universe. This made sense to me because it explained
what happened to Dad *in very loose* terms. But what it really did was open
my eyes to the fact that it is not religion or God that I dislike, as I had
thought for most of my life. What I realized was that I truly hated and
was disgusted with what "man" has done with and to religion. With this
in mind I have begun to open myself up to all of the religions of the world.
In this attempt I have also tried to find a commonality between the ones
I know of. The commonality I have found is that they teach that we
should all live "good" lives. By this I mean that we should lose our
self-importance and realize that we are all one, and that we are all equal.
Each religion has its own prescribed way in which we should accomplish
this. To this I say fine, there's more than one way to skin a cat. It's the
results that are important. How you lived your life and treated others, not
who you pray to or how often.

In class discussions, many students are quite outspoken about their
criticisms and rejection of institutional religion. This is a contrast to
those students who affirm such religion, but are hesitant to speak up and
defend their allegiance. Of special note, however, is that the vast
majority of students affirm a personal faith in "spirituality." When
described, this spirituality tends to be anti-institution, more grounded
in Eastern and nature religions, and is typically talked about in Jungian
and feminist terms.

Typical student criticisms of religion include the following. Many
people use religion as a way to feel good and to be preoccupied with
Heaven and their own salvation at the expense of a suffering world,
largely ignored. Many of the "religious" are taken by their own righteousness and use this to sit in judgment over others. There is a strong
in-group/out-group assertion that is used to condemn whole groups of
people as evil or hopeless. This can be related to political and racial
differences, to sexual preferences, to nonconformity with cultural
norms (criminals, the insane), and to issues of poverty and unemploy-
ment (wherein success and achievement are viewed as divine rewards
for virtuous living). In addition to sweet sentimentality and hypocritical
intolerance, there is the co-option of religion by political groups and by
the particular values of a society. So religion is used to support the
individualism and competition of a capitalist country or the government
programs of control in socialist countries—that is, the moral majority

and liberation theology. Another criticism is aimed at the deadness of overritualized religion, which has accounted for radically declining church attendance in England.

In a classroom situation, I present a series of statements for purposes of discussion. I happen to believe these ideas are true, but present them for the purpose of stimulating discussion. See how you (and your partner) respond to these propositions.

(1) There are ultimate truths cutting across all cultures.

(2) Evil is a force in its own right, capable of affecting individuals and groups.

(3) Believing religious social workers need a God who is present in the midst of human suffering.

(4) God is not only merciful, but at times anguished and outraged.

(5) God is personal, although seemingly elusive and unpredictable.

(6) People can know what God wants and can contribute to his work.

(7) We are not abandoned in this world, but may be empowered by spirit.

(8) There are varied routes to God, including nonreligious searches for truth.

Since I have already mentioned in this book ideas stemming from existential philosophy and Eastern religions, and since most of our economically deprived and minority clients come from a Judeo-Christian heritage, it would seem appropriate to summarize what seems special about this religious tradition. The Judeo-Christian heritage asserts that there is a personal God who has been and currently remains involved in the sufferings of people. God, from this perspective, revealed Himself through the sufferings and struggles of the Hebrew people and eventually in the person of Jesus. Jesus demonstrated himself as a unique personality and affirmed the persons he encountered as individual, valued personalities. He affirmed an eternal possibility for individual persons, not by returning to a nebulous sea of universal spirit, but by entering the Kingdom of God, wherein individual uniqueness would be somehow preserved and affirmed. Both the mercy and the judgment of God interact in this world of human destinies. The person of Jesus has been upheld by Christians as singularly divine in nature. His resurrection after death demonstrated the hope of personal salvation and eternal life. This hope has been a stabilizing force for masses of people enduring seemingly unchangeable oppression and suffering.

Franz Rosenzweig believed Judaism and Christianity to be the two most true religions for modern human beings (Borowitz, 1966, chap. 3). He did not see these two as contradictory, nor was there any need for a merger. According to Rosenzweig, the Jew is born with that which the Christian must acquire, for the Jew is placed in a living relationship with God at birth. The Jew continues a historical experience, a continuing covenant nurtured by the Law. For the non-Jew, Christianity can also be an effective means to God.

Religion in America has certainly been demonstrating a resurgence of healthy vitality. If one accepts the premise that there are varied routes to God, this also implies numerous modes of experiencing spiritual realities within a particular religious faith. Religion offers not only hope, but different means of surviving the alienation and value confusions of modern society. Even the in-group emphasis need not be linked with intolerance. It often reflects a positive dynamic by which groups of a common mind-set can experience a healing power of shared belief and loyalty among those who worship, suffer, enjoy, and pray together. A society dominated by the powerful value forces of its economic and political systems needs a counterbalancing value force that is based in a moral system. Organized religions in dialogue with one another can potentially provide this important third force.

Organized religion suffers from the same self-deceptions and power maneuvers as any organized human institution. Yet its very premises nurture a correcting self-critique. Many of the existential philosophers, playwrights, novelists, artists, and poets represent a religious vitality. Not only do they expose our popularly accepted illusions of progress through rationalism, technology, organized programs of social control, and narrowly oversimplified sociological and psychological panaceas, but they point to the very difficulties we have in knowing God. Our sense of reverence, awe, wonder, and the poetic has been seriously crippled by societal forces. We succumb to this throughout the meandering of our daily affairs. Our need for an absolute is a submerged, gnawing hunger distorted into an array of addictions, idolized relationships, and empty illusions of achievement and security. Who is God? Can we know Him/Her in our modern world? That "hound of heaven" pants within us not only with intensity, but with ferocity.

Discussions about religion invariably arrive at the question of authority versus tolerance. Most social work students have a healthy rebellious streak that challenges dogmatic and tyrannical authority. All religions have some creed, or definition of faith, that affirms ultimate truths. Most philosophies, too, affirm specific ultimate truths. We also value tolerance and pluralism with respect to differing religious and philosophical truths. This has been our historical heritage in America. Does tolerance require the relativization of all values, as has become the popular stance in modern society?

Judeo-Christian thought makes a simple and straightforward case for religious authority. The human mind is finite, and therefore cannot grasp truths that are infinite in nature. Therefore, it is necessary that divine revelations teach human beings the nature of the infinite, and what the infinite expects of humans. C. S. Lewis, in *The Abolition of Man* (1947), sets forth the similarity of ultimate truths revealed through the many world religions. Jung (1958) conveys a similar position as a result of his lengthy research of the symbols and myths set forth by the varied religions. If one believes that the authority of ultimate truths is revealed through all lasting religions, there would appear to be no problem with tolerance of different faiths.

Classical philosophers, such as the Stoics, Socrates, Plato, and Aristotle, differed with the above assertion that the finite mind could not grasp infinite truth. They believed that human reason could arrive at a knowledge of ultimate truth and of what was expected of human beings from a perspective of "natural law." Again we have an affirmation of ultimate authority and standards for humankind. Judeo-Christian belief has, on occasion, accepted the natural-law premises of the classical philosophers. This is found most notably in the writings of Thomas Aquinas. The central theme of Allan Bloom's *The Closing of the American Mind* (1987) is a challenge to the current vogue of relativism. Bloom recommends a solid study of the classic philosophers.

In your self-study, you have discovered how the subjective process of world design can be transcended by experiences labeled as freedom, peak experiences, and archetypes. It is one thing to refer to these occurrences as spiritual. It is quite another matter to understand the meaning of these events and provide them some direction. This is where the matter of having some ultimate truth perspective, beyond your self-created world design, becomes exceedingly important. Without it, you either dismiss the value of such spiritual experiences or conclude that you are having divine revelations. Both positions can be equally dangerous and deceptive.

How important is the integration of your religious/philosophical beliefs with your subjective experience and your views on theory? Let us suppose that your passion is directed by your will and your will is rooted in your view of life. A religion defines a view of life and provides truths, myths, symbols, and historical incidents that may well arouse your passions as a result of your otherwise empty and hungry will. Faith is not a matter of intellectual allegiance, but of a personal relationship with some conception of truth that is both within and beyond yourself. The same could be said for philosophy's relation to truth. One's religious faith is a presence, a love for God, a standing in the light of truth.

In this sense, religion/philosophy offers us an ever-present opportunity to step outside the reoccurring boundaries of our world design security images. Religion/philosophy can also be misused as a means of supporting one's world design. Since not only you but your clients may be freed or defensively reinforced by religion/philosophy, it becomes important to see how these factors are integrated with your practice theories and your sense of self.

As we look at our clients' religions, we may wonder how there can be several seemingly opposing ideas concerning religious practices even within one religion. This is true not only among the obvious variety of Protestant denominations, but among Jews, Catholics, and Buddhists as well. One explanation is offered by Scott Peck (1987) in his discussion of the four stages of spiritual development, found in his recent book *The Different Drum*. These stages, according to Peck, are as follows:

(1) chaotic, antisocial
(2) formal, institutional
(3) skeptic, individual
(4) mystic, communal

Peck presents a model of how to develop and sustain communities of people. He believes that the differing phases of development account for the marked variations apparent among religious people. But he also maintains that it is possible for these differing perspectives to coexist within a community. His perspective on not only tolerance but the affirmation of understanding of such differences would be useful to any helping professional.

Consider the possible dilemmas students may face in practice. How does a student handle the religious beliefs of a client when they appear to be reinforcing the problem of concern? When a client declares that central to his or her problems is a loss of faith, or of meaning in life, what can a student do? When is it appropriate and useful to share one's personal faith or philosophy with a client? When one's personal beliefs conflict with a client's life choice, what does one do? Is praying with a client ever appropriate?

Without a degree of comfort as well as some acquaintance with varied religious/philosophical perspectives, how can you respond to such challenges? You have no doubt noted your own discomfort in addressing such matters even in discussions of religion or philosophy with your friends and relatives.

I have found it useful to underscore the social systems model of social work in relation to these kinds of questions. If a client has family or friends who share in his or her belief system, it is preferable that matters of belief be discussed with them rather than with the worker alone. The worker may even offer to facilitate such a discussion if the client prefers this. If the client is a part of a church or synagogue community, he or she has the ready resources available of fellow believers and a rabbi, priest, or minister. At times a phone contact made by the worker to the church leader may be important in order to help clarify the questions that have arisen for the client. If a worker has the same faith as the client, he or she may share personal interpretations or understandings, but should do so as a peer and not as a helping expert. If you would like to know more about religious practices different from your own, to understand your clients' spiritual experiences better, a useful undertaking is to visit church or synagogue services, Indian ceremonials, revival meetings, and so on. This is far more useful than reading about differences in faiths, although such reading is a helpful supplement.

Pain is a more common human experience than pleasure. While most of us may not be aware of living lives of "quiet desperation," we are quite aware that experiences of happiness tend to be transient and elusive. On the other hand, experiences of "hanging in there," of "getting by," of "trying to keep on top of things," and of a reoccurring dullness anticipating something better predominate. We are more often overwhelmed with demands and expectations, disappointments, and confusion than we are by wonder, ecstasy, intimacy, and beauty. We strive hard to build in a few of those positives when we can.

We seek pleasures regularly, but they seldom result in what we think of as happiness. Pleasure, as a matter of fact, tends to lead us into other forms of pain. Living in the midst of a culture that hawks pleasure at every turn, we find it most difficult simply to accept pleasures as passing feelings. Pleasures become the stimuli for comparisons, worries, regrets, hopes, demands, and obsessions. When pleasures are put in the context of repeated and secured experiences of our world design interests, they tend toward both disappointments and eventual dullness.

Pain or suffering, on the other hand, can be the basis of human compassion, providing a common human bond that crosses cultures, politics, and racial and sexual differences. Human suffering is a common point of departure in our search for religious and philosophical truth. Our insufficiency is God's opportunity, as the saying goes. Humiliation can lead to reconciliation; the wayward son returns home. Our most profound suffering, according to Ernest Becker (1973), is our awareness of death. It is this awareness that existentially challenges our personal illusions of independent autonomy and control over life.

Chapter 9

BECOMING A SOJOURNER

At this point on the road to practice wisdom, our trails divide. They may continue on separately, and they may cross one another now and then. You will, in time, find other trails running close and parallel to your own, and those following them will be welcome brothers and sisters on your trip. In this chapter I will briefly review our journey and suggest tools and disciplines for your continued venture.

We began by exploring our personal subjectivity. We used as markers notions of passion, memory, freedom (integration-creation), and archetypes. Our focus took the form of identity development termed *security images* or *world designs*. This was elaborated by a description of how our personal need for protective hideouts resonates well with social reinforcements through the roles we take. These reinforcers include our families, relatives, friends, social groupings, professional positions, sexual and cultural linkages, and being citizens in an economic-political order. The arts and entertainment media and the world of academia play no small role in offering us appealing images and conclusions to reinforce our prized world designs. We came to appreciate, too, how powerful and even automatic is the guiding force of our repetitive world design. We realized, with some discomfort, just how deceptive and manipulative this force can be in its protection of some of our own needs for grandiosity, righteousness, and escape. We noted how world design, as a natural and necessary component of individual identity, sometimes impaired our own growth as well as our ability to understand and work effectively with our clients.

Yet beyond this closely guarded world design we found a capacity within us to transcend these conclusions. We could experience a freedom in our awareness and in our sensitive use of reason to generate an openness to both our engaging world and the creative-integrative prompting from within ourselves. We even found some welcome signposts to support us in our own positive archetype images.

This discovery of our own freedom had its immediate application to how we use ourselves in professional helping roles. The image of detached caring enabled us to appreciate more fully the client before us, so that we need not hide behind our theoretical categories. We appreciated our own need for an engaging vitality as an ideal way of responding to the problems and issues a client presents. The complex jungle of competing theories and related techniques could be tamed and effectively utilized through the very manner in which we related to a client. Not only did our vitality provide us with a means to deal with a client's present motivations, but we also discovered how our own creative process often enables us to select appropriate techniques.

This emphasis upon personal subjectivity in no way diminishes the importance of knowledge to be pursued. The value of varied ideas among personality and social system theories remains crucial. So, too, is the import of learning and using a variety of techniques. Without this armamentarium of knowledge and skills our inner creative-integrative process would remain narrow and insufficient to the task of helping the variety of people with whom we work. Yet this accumulation of knowledge and skill is a lifelong professional endeavor.

Your limited know-how, as a student, need not deter your use of the practice wisdom orientation. We are simply challenging a professional myth: that theory is what directs practice. This myth has resulted in the erroneous absolutizing and idolizing of theory. We have been tempted to believe our theories to be true rather than of a relative nature. Knowledge in the social sciences has not proven itself as it has in the physical or hard sciences. If we are of a scientific inclination, we should at least begin our search for theoretical truth by an acceptance of current research evidence of theory and practice insufficiencies (Krill, 1986, chap. 3). On the other hand, it is likely that the human sciences may never achieve the exact predictability of the hard sciences. In either case we are well advised to replace the professional myth on theory with a different idea: Practice is informed by your personal integration of theories (and related skills) with your religious and philosophical perspectives, and all of these with your personal subjective experience. Theory may challenge your subjective experience and vice versa. Religion/philosophy may challenge theory and vice versa. Subjectivity may challenge religion/philosophy and vice versa. Practice itself is an extension of your subjective process, for subjective experience is engaging and interactive with the world.

This complexity of knowledge does not require you to compose some all-inclusive theory, any more than it requires you to master all theories. Nor does this call for a diminishment of your own religious faith or philosophical beliefs. You may well choose a theoretical framework and personal belief system that best suits your present needs and life orientation. Your task, then, is one of refinement and expansion of understanding so as to modify limiting ideas and be more inclusive of other ideas and experiences. Such is the nature of theory building and of maturation in one's faith. The pursuit of truth is openness to the new as well as validating important truths of the past, including the ancient past. Bloom's *The Closing of the American Mind* (1987) makes a strong case for seeing the human sciences and popular philosophies as having gone astray in a destructive manner principally because they failed to build upon the sources of wisdom from our historical heritage. Social sciences built a tower of knowledge upon weak, narrow, and insufficient underpinnings and the tendency is for this Tower of Babel to defend and insulate itself. Your freedom as a budding professional is to realize this and be willing to part company with questionable dogmatic assertions. The social work profession in particular has been prone to ignoring its own disinterest in philosophy while embracing a seductive array of pragmatic techniques and political passions. We become victims of our own ideologies, which too often blossom forth as conspiratorial thinking. When you link up with a conspiracy or ideology you trade your personal integrity for the social imprisonment of your own world design.

DIRECTION FOR YOUR PERSONAL PATH

Keeping a journal, or "journaling," can serve as self-therapy as well as creating a resource bank for creative thinking and a valued record of your personal and professional life. Journaling of this kind is like keeping a diary—both very positive and troubling experiences are worthy of notation. It is useful to keep a record of how you have handled problems and frustrations in new ways. A journal permits a constructive use of thought that may otherwise be dissipated by inner chatter. In journaling, you may speculate as to the meaning of dreams, of confusing or upsetting events, of unusual and discomforting reactions to situations. You can record creative or speculative new ideas that may form the seeds of later development. As you anticipate a challenge or are embroiled by upsetting emotions, you can look back over your journal to similar situations recorded and often find helpful direction. Your summations of characteristics you have appreciated about yourself and hints of budding potentials you have recorded can be quite helpful at moments of low self-esteem and or failure.

Meditation is a most helpful daily exercise for an experience of reentering, or affirming, a positive and grounded sense of oneself. Meditation opens one up to those healing facets of one's subjective life that are not run by habitual inner chatter. Meditation, too, can be a self-therapy, as one allows unfinished business to surface in one's awareness.

Daily readings are important as a further way of expanding one's perspectives on life. These readings should be of people one respects and from whom one wants to learn. One may even discover a brotherhood or sisterhood of people who share those views of life that you prize, but seldom talk about with others. It is best that you set a special time for such readings. Many people prefer mornings, prior to any exposure to the newspaper, radio, or television, or before they assess the worries of the day.

As indicated above, your course of professional studies, continued postgraduate reading, and use of workshops and seminars are your main vehicles for acquiring, critiquing, and expanding professional knowledge. But all of this will become rigidified or chaotic nonsense if you do not value the experiential learning provided you through the lives and struggles of your clients. If you lose direct client contact by becoming an administrator, supervisor, planner, researcher, or academician, then you had better supplement your job with some private or voluntary direct-helping activity. Interpersonal relationships with peers and others of the hierarchy are insufficient for the learning needed from those who suffer and whom we are committed to help as social workers.

Chapter 10

APPLICATION FOR
TRAINING OF LAYPEOPLE

Many of the exercises and related ideas you have explored in relation to practice wisdom can be adapted for laypeople. Professional helpers as well as students in employee assistance programs (EAPs), church-related agencies, and community centers are acting as educators for laypeople. The final three chapters in this volume provide a description of the design and focus of self-awareness training that has special appeal to a growing number of laypeople. I have used this model successfully with EAPs.

EMPLOYEE ASSISTANCE PROGRAMS

Stress management and the promotion of self-esteem have been two of the most popular aims of EAP training. These two hopes for personal improvement are frequently tied to problem management. Problems of most concern to employers, naturally, are those that impede productiveness on the job. Burnout and addiction have long been at the top of the list of such problems. These two problems have been so often discussed, lectured on, and written about that a sizable number of employees would admit to one or the other of the difficulties, although their actual symptoms may not yet be at a level of interference with work performance. So a seminar addressing both burnout and addiction themes can be expected to attract employees.

There is another attractive feature of this joint theme for EAPs: the notion of spirituality. I know of a large company that seeks to maintain high employee morale through "three pillars": physical fitness, stress management, and spirituality. This company has no difficulty providing for the first two of these, using a gym, organized sports, and seminars. It has been at a loss as to how to deal with spirituality. This deficit is not surprising when one considers that even among staffs of helping professionals affiliated with religious group-sponsored agencies, discussions of personal spirituality are too often carefully avoided in staff development programs. In a company where no particular religious connection is apparent, there is considerable discomfort in dealing with spirituality issues. The concept of "freedom of religious belief" tends to result in careful avoidance of any talk of religion.

While a sizable percentage of the American population are church members, a very small number of these people are involved in small discussion groups aimed at clarifying personal beliefs. Outside of churches and universities there are virtually no opportunities for people to share and struggle together with their religious and philosophical beliefs. Too often, one is not in a university at the time in life when the greatest need for spiritual reflection is experienced (typically at midlife). One may not feel ready to link with a particular church, and, even if one did, there may be no opportunity for personal sharing and struggle over beliefs with fellow church members. Too often, ministers are comfortable in the authority role but uneasy in a facilitative role in relation to varied beliefs.

The seminar on burnout and addiction leads people to consider new explanations for their difficulty. Rather than seeing the trouble as a behavior that must be changed or desensitized, or as requiring a shift in one's type of work, this double-theme seminar focuses upon important personal beliefs and values. Much like practice wisdom's call for an integration of subjective experiences with philosophy/religion and with theory, the burnout-addiction seminar seeks a greater awareness as to one's everyday beliefs (surfacing spontaneously with pain and anxiety) and the larger ideals one may use to guide one's life (religious and philosophical beliefs). Seminars addressing spirituality directly, yet without representing a particular dogmatic viewpoint, can help people better formulate their own ideals and then move out to active church or synagogue membership or an association with others whose philosophy they may share.

In order to clarify the interrelationship between burnout and addiction and to relate the two to personal beliefs, I will share the description of the seminar as provided to employees. This is a detailed explanation because employees need to have a clear sense as to how this seminar differs from other programs addressing similar topics. The following description is sent to all employees, along with the date of the seminar.

ADDICTION AND BURNOUT: DEFIERS OF CHANGE

Two of the most common forms of stress in the work world today are burnout and addiction. There is a common factor basic to both of the problems. Why are addictions so hard to change? Because of the presence of dominating powerful *desires*. Why is it so difficult to generate enthusiasm in a condition of burnout? Because of the lack of energizing *desires*. To understand the nature and origin of one's desires is to provide an important handle for dealing with problems of both addiction and burnout.

Few, if any, of us are free from addictions. You might define an addiction as being controlled by some behavior that you once valued, but now believe to be bad for you. Frequently someone else brings the negative effects of your addiction to your attention and then you reflect upon it for some time before declaring it "bad." Usually there are a few trial runs at giving it up before you realize just how powerful a habit it has become.

It is reassuring to point the finger at "falling-down drunks" or "screaming drug addicts" while at the same time resting comfortably with one's own addictions of smoking, caffeine, tranquilizers, aspirin, TV watching, gossiping, overwork, preoccupation with worry or achieving success, overeating, "relaxation drinking," making money, sexual compulsions, or whatever.

The same is true about burnout. While our usual idea of burnout is the image of the exhausted or continually bored employee, there is another form of burnout that is often described as "mid-life crisis." This is the "Peggy Lee" syndrome: "Is that all there is?" We have followed a set of passionate pursuits to a point of disappointment. The only reason this disillusioning process is termed "mid-life crisis" is because of our present culture of enticing escape routes. Our chase after false hopes tends to go on until we are between 40 and 50. This treadmill of alternating pursuits takes a variety of forms: job changes, more education, affairs and serial marriages, more kids or pets, relocations, changing forms of recreation, self-development and awareness programs, more material possessions and entertainments. When there is a lack of lasting satisfaction in any of these we try to build in our own relief from despair with one or more of the addictive behaviors aforementioned.

Certainly there is nothing wrong with desire; it is the spice of life. But both addiction and burnout have to do with a growing exclusiveness of a desire. We put all our eggs in one basket and neglect other needs and desires available to us. From excitement we move toward dullness; from freedom toward compulsion.

Several interesting questions emerge from the dilemmas of addiction and burnout. Why is it so difficult to change a troubling desire? Why is it equally difficult to generate motivational desires in the grip of burnout? Is there a point in the pursuit of desire when we can assert a perspective of moderation? Is desire solely a product of powerful instincts or social forces (advertising, media seductions)? Can we change a habit pattern, whether of addiction or burnout, without also changing our life-style and belief system in some critical way? Does it do any good to substitute a new desire pattern for a former, troubling one?

In this two-part workshop you will explore how desires that begin as innocent wishes may end up as troubling obsessions, compulsions, and addictions. You will be invited to identify problematic habit patterns of your own and learn how they are expressions of your personal belief system. Signs of burnout or addiction commonly reveal a life-style (and related personal beliefs) that seems contradictory to the ideals we uphold. This inner contradiction can mar our sense of integrity and provoke guilt.

Desire can be as hard to start (burnout) as it is hard to stop (addiction). There are large numbers of people making good livings from either claiming to be able to motivate others or promising to free others from compulsive desires. An important issue to be developed in this workshop will be that of how beliefs are changed. Too often they are not changed but only redirected to equally troubling patterns. The result is a continuing emotional roller coaster.

An important lesson in the transformation of desire is to be found in the tale of Scrooge, told by Charles Dickens in *A Christmas Carol*. The attainment of freedom from controlling problematic desires or deadening habit patterns is a matter of confronting some ultimate questions as to one's life direction. A change in life-style also calls for a change in whom you allow to influence your belief systems. While this workshop proposes no particular ideal belief system, it does address the process of change and seeks to inspire participants toward a fresh search.

———

This descriptive statement has brought in double the usual number of employees who ordinarily attend seminars open to anyone in a company. Perhaps this is a result of the double content of both addiction and burnout. It has also proved to be a safe description insofar as it arouses interest without divulging the key ideas to be presented. The danger of plagiarism by enterprising company personnel, for use in developing their own seminar of a similar nature, is satisfactorily controlled.

MARKETING SEMINARS

A seminar description such as the above will be of value only as a follow-up to a personal visit to whoever coordinates such programs in a company. You must sell the idea for the seminar on the basis of what you already know, or can surmise, about the specific needs of a company or helping agency. With a company, the usual concern is productivity on the part of all employees. Issues of burnout and addiction are related to common company problems of morale, self-esteem, and stress management.

Whenever you conduct a seminar, it is important to provide evaluation sheets for the learners. These can later be used as evidence of the seminar's impact in selling the program to another agency.

Following a seminar it is also important that you meet again with the coordinator who organized the seminar, for the purpose of evaluating together the results of the program. You should also use this meeting to learn from the coordinator the names of any other companies or agencies he or she knows that might be interested in a similar program. Naturally, you need to obtain the names of key people to contact in these recommended agencies.

FORMAT OF TRAINING

The time factor can vary considerably for these seminars. Possibilities can include a single hour-long introductory presentation, although this is hardly adequate to cover the content. An hour's presentation might be an interim step between a talk with the coordinator and the full seminar presentation. It is used when the coordinator wants to involve employees in the decision as to whether or not they wish to pursue a full seminar.

The seminar itself, as described in the next two chapters, requires three hours. This may be done as a half-day presentation or on two separate occasions of one and one-half hours each. If the company desires a full day or a weekend workshop, the presentations can be extended in a most vital way by incorporating some of the exercises described for use with follow-up self-help groups (Chapter 13).

The self-help follow-up groups are an option offered in the basic seminar. The two types of self-help groups I have proposed are a Belief Exploration Group and a Workaholics Group. The seminar itself opens people to the idea of reexamining some of their important values. This is clearly a personal undertaking in the area of spirituality and/or philosophical search. Many participants will prefer to do this privately, through reading, prayer, and meditation. Others will utilize available support groups such as their own churches or women's groups. There will be some, however, who would like to continue the search begun in the seminar with their fellow employees. Or they may not have an existing support group, yet prefer to continue their spiritual quest in the company of others. The Belief Exploration Group meets these needs.

The Workaholic Group is based essentially on an adaptation of the 12-step program of Alcoholics Anonymous. There is existing literature as to how these steps may be reformulated for nonalcoholics.

The leadership style for seminars and follow-up groups can vary according to the leader's preference. Personally, I have found an ideal style, when doing seminars alone, is to engage the audience as rapidly as possible with questions designed to generate personal sharing. Another useful method for maintaining a high level of vitality is to have coleaders who take turns and freely interrupt one another. It seems wise to me to choose a coleader with characteristics (age, sex, communication style) quite different from yourself. The follow-up groups should use coleaders, so as to model a quality of sharing and respecting differences for the group members. The Workaholic Group should move toward becoming leaderless, in true self-help group fashion, after ten or twelve meetings.

In the next chapter we will examine the handling of the first half of the seminar.

Chapter 11

THE DESIRE SPIRAL

The presentation of ideas and exercises in this chapter and the next will follow the format used in seminars for laypeople, such as in employee assistance programs. We begin by defining both addiction and burnout in their expanded versions, as presented in Chapter 10. Audience involvement is sought almost from the start by inviting members to suggest further examples of both addiction and burnout in addition to what you have already stated.

Next the linkage is clarified between addiction and burnout on the basis of desire. With burnout there seems to be a lack of desire—one cannot even generate desire. With addiction, desire has become uncontrollable, one cannot stop it. The example of a workaholic illustrates one way in which burnout and addiction exist together. A person's primary life energy is devoted to work, so that the rest of his or her life experience becomes quite an uninteresting secondary matter. Yet the intense pursuit of this desire to work as much as possible commonly results in exhaustion, a sense of profound dissatisfaction, and even failure, and this may be termed burnout.

What is desire, and how do we experience it? (Here we are looking for an existential rather than a psychological definition.) Seminar participants may be invited to respond to these questions, or to expand on the leader's ideas. Generally, this discussion produces such reflections as these: Desire is vitality, a driving intent, a sense of heightened connection with one's environment. Desire makes life worthwhile and heightens one's sense of individuality. Desire can also be risky and scary and one may feel pushed into interests opposed to one's values. Desire can be a threat.

At this point participants may be asked to jot down three needs or desires that seem to be powerful influences in their lives at the present time. These are to be desires that, if unsatisfied, would cause much frustration. As the participants do this, the leader draws the diagram shown in Figure 11.1 on a board or flip chart. The desire spiral is then presented somewhat as follows.

Desires begin as innocent wishes, where we are playing with some area of potential interest. If we wish to pursue a wish, we move to wanting. Here we become serious about putting forth energy and thought as to how to satisfy a desire. When a desire reaches the next level, we have declared it a need, and therefore especially important to us. Here is where self-pity may enter in, when satisfaction of the desire fails to occur. By the time desire reaches the level of demanding, we have made it centrally important to our sense of self-esteem. If someone interferes with our desired satisfaction at this point, we will become angry. If we find ourselves deprived of the desired satisfaction we will likely become depressed. We have now defined our notion of happiness, in part, by satisfaction of this desire. Continued intensification, or idolization, of the desire may result in obsession. At the level of obsession, the desire is determining our subjective life. We have limited interest in the world at large unless situations relate directly to our desire. Our awareness and life perspectives have become rigidly narrow and exclusive, the very opposite of the sense of freedom and expansiveness we experienced at the first level of innocent and playful wishing. Finally, when a desire reaches the level of addiction one is often wishing to be rid of it. The desire now appears harmful to us or to others and is clearly interfering with our life in some way. Yet we cannot stop it, for its power seems to dominate and possess us. We feel as if we have fully *become* our desire, such as the person addicted to alcohol who refers to him- or herself as "an alcoholic." Examples from the teacher's own life experience, or from people with whom he or she is familiar, may be used to illustrate the differing levels of the desire spiral.

The two cone shapes in the figure illustrate two forms of spirals as they apply to the conceptualization. The inverted cone illustrates the spiral that moves from desire as expansiveness toward narrowed exclusiveness. The upright spiral illustrates the spiral that moves from mild interest toward greater and greater intensity, ending in possession.

Audience members are asked to reflect upon particular desires of their own that have worked their way up on the spiral to a point where

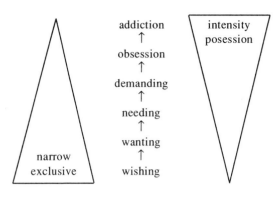

Figure 11.1 The Desire Spiral

they have become problematic or at least worrisome. The teacher continues to elaborate the concept of the desire spiral and then invites questions and comments before inquiring about people's personal issues regarding problematic desires.

One useful clarification for the leader to make is the relation of burnout to the desire spiral. Here are two connections. First, when a desire reaches the levels of obsession or addiction one can find oneself exhausted by both the mental energy expended and the physical effects on the body. At the same time, the very narrowing of interest in life apart from the desire can produce a dullness; the repetition of the habit pattern tends toward boredom. What began as vitality and spontaneity is now a much less satisfying activity. These are the ingredients of burnout. Second, a person who becomes fearful of strongly desiring anything may burn him- or herself out by inhibiting even the earliest phases of desire. The catatonic is an extreme example—one who sits like a statue, entertaining no wishes or wants. This, too, is burnout of a sort, for the individual has become totally hopeless about desiring in general.

Another useful clarification is an exposure of the illusional quality of desire. The experiences in a concentration camp described by Victor Frankl are of special note. Prisoners were immediately deprived of almost all possessions, opportunities, and activities that had previously been personally satisfying. They experienced losses through changes in diet, work, relationships, clothing, personal appearance, time management, even their very homes. Frankl describes these horrors as a loss of

life meanings. Some gave up and soon died; others were able to construct new meanings in order to continue and endure. Still others
already were living by meanings that transcended these primary losses.

A further clarification the leader may make is to suggest that as the
participants reflect upon potentially or actual problematic desires, they
will also become aware that they have many desires in their lives, most
of which probably have never become problematic. Why is it that some
desires ascend the spiral of becoming problems or worries while other
desires do not?

Seminar participants are then divided into small groups to share
reactions with one another. Their discussions may include responses to
any of these questions:

- What brought you to this seminar?
- Is there a problematic desire or lack of desire you wish to share?
- Why do some desires become problematic while others do not?

Groupings should be no larger than four or five participants, so each
person has an opportunity to speak. Time allotment for this activity can
be 15-20 minutes. The point of these discussions is to engage people
with one another and thereby generate feedback for a total group
discussion.

The total group discussion following the small groups is an opportunity to clarify questions, reactions, challenges, and personal experiences as they relate to the desire spiral idea. Here are some typical
issues raised by an audience.

- "I experience my addiction as a 'quick fix' so that I can get on with my
  normal life activities." This suggests that an addiction, such as that to
  caffeine, tobacco, or sugar, does not appear to be a narrowing of life
  interest, but rather a support to continued engagement with life. One does
  not experience any obsession unless deprived of the satisfaction desired.
  With regular satisfactions one can arrive at the addictive level without ever
  having experienced the levels of demanding or obsession.
- "When I satisfy a 'want' and the result is disappointing, or fairly neutral, I
  do not pursue that desire. Even if I occasionally follow it again, It never
  gets beyond 'wanting.'" This observation suggests that moderation of
  desire interest is related to the meaning one attaches to the satisfaction
  experience. Some desires may be declared pleasant and are easily "let go,"
  while others may be seen as so pleasurable or comforting that they appear
  to be discoveries on the route to happiness.
- "The desires that become strong for me seem related to my early life
  history. I was deprived of some things when growing up, and those very

things have become extremely important to me now." Here we see that meanings constructed in childhood become strong stimulants for specific desire pursuits in adulthood. One may have lived with poverty and now is extremely invested in money, physical possessions, and security. Another grew up with prohibitions concerning sex or alcohol, and these have emerged into enticing adult pursuits.

- "Addictions seem to have a strange way of feeding upon themselves. The more you do it, the more you seem to need to do it . . . even when you are disgusted with what you do." It is useful to clarify how this process occurs. As one's desire moves to a level of limiting one's interests in the surrounding world, one's natural growth process becomes impaired. We grow psychologically and spiritually through ongoing and expanded contacts with the world around us. As we reduce this activity, we experience a loss, a lack, sometimes even a dullness because of the lack of engagement. This very lack incites a hunger for *more*. But the "more" is not specified, so it takes the form of increased desire for our object of addiction. We pursue our prized desire all the more fervently, thereby further limiting our interest and a sense of lack.

- "Aren't some addictions purely physical? What about inherited predispositions? I've heard that some folks can become addicted with their first drink." Here we have another important clarification. Some addictions appear to be entirely physical and others emotional. The question of what is learned and what is inherited, or strictly a chemical-physiological condition, is often a murky issue. Closely related to this is the question of whether or not the body is a key factor. Some people seem to pursue a strong desire throughout their lives without ever becoming addicts in the sense of losing control and wanting to stop. Others seem to indulge moderately for a period of time and suddenly find themselves "hooked." These observations appear to negate the validity of the desire spiral concept. On the other hand, we may simply be pinpointing differences as to what factors set off a dominating desire. For some this may be purely physical; for others it may be emotional or social, which may or may not be related to childhood experiences; for still others there is a combination of all these factors. The meaning one attaches to the problematic desire and the challenge of how to handle it remain important factors.

- "We live in an addictive society. We're all taught from little up to chase the carrot on the stick. It's how we motivate our kids. It's what makes a consumer society work. We are reinforced every day of our lives by the TV, the advertisements, and by our friends and jobs. There's no avoiding this." Here is another very useful premise. Addictions and burnout are not simply individual matters. They are an expression of the context in which we live. The powerful inclinations within ourselves interact constantly with powerful reinforcing norms, expectations, and enticements outside ourselves.

This segment of the seminar is rich in discussion. The use of varied groups and the three focal questions provides responses in the total group that are both personal and theoretical. This allows for elaborate discussion as to the nature and complexities of addiction and burnout. Depending on the time allotted for the first seminar period, this discussion segment may range from 15 minutes to well over an hour.

THE DILEMMAS OF CHANGE

At any point the leader may move the discussion in a new direction, in preparation for anticipating the second seminar session. In doing this, the leader introduces the following ideas: It is one thing to understand how addictions and burnout arise, but it is quite another matter to change them. What happens when you try to give up an addiction? Or what happens when you try to motivate yourself when you are feeling burned out? Or what happens when you try to get someone else to give up an addiction, or you want to motivate someone beyond their burnout?

These questions invite participants as a total group to share some of the specific frustrations, fears, and failures that usually are related to their attending this seminar. The discussion is handled in such a way as to emphasize and accept the common experiences of floundering or "being stuck" and unable to change.

A common response is that of inner conflict: One wants to change, yet there seems to be a part of oneself that will not change. The result is usually guilt. Strangely enough, one can feel guilt whether or not one successfully changes an unwanted behavior. If one gives up an addictive behavior there is commonly an odd guilt—that of no longer being true to some part of oneself. Once, one had spontaneously chosen this desire because one valued it, and now one is giving it up. If this change is because someone else is complaining about the addiction, rather than primarily oneself, one may feel that loss of the desire satisfaction is a betrayal of oneself. On the other hand, if one does not give up the addiction, one feels guilt because one is hurting oneself or someone else, or not being true to one's reasoned decision to stop the addiction.

Inner conflicts provide a wealth of rationalization as well as catastrophic expectations. The consequences of such change may be more than one can bear, perhaps worse than the results of continued addiction. One's friends and family may experience threat over such change. Addictive behavior is often a mutually satisfying social activity. Others may feel betrayed or, at best, may lose interest in you.

If one succeeds in stopping an addiction, one soon finds oneself substituting a new addiction, one that may not be even recognized as an addiction for some time to come. It may end up a worse addiction, more damaging to one's health or to one's relationships than the previous one.

Another common occurrence with the ending of some addictive behavior is the suppression of the strong desire. The desire is not really modified, only the behavior itself. Suppressed desires, powerful in nature, will often take their toll in other ways. One may become increasingly irritable, depressed, self-righteous, boring, temperamental, or even violent. How much of this can significant others put up with? Can one continue to live with this new self?

A "power of positive thinking" approach to overcoming burnout may easily result in a troubling sense of inner contradiction. One feels at war with oneself in an effort to demonstrate success to the world. The sense of deception is keenly felt, and the guilt and related depression must also be hidden. One feels a failure within, a liar without. The cycle may continue to a point where the outer facade no longer is possible. Then one's failure goes public and one feels even worse.

Perhaps the most common concern of most pop psychologies today is self-esteem. A frequent misperception about low self-esteem is that it is derived from deprivation and emotional traumas of childhood. Hobart Mowrer (1961) has a far more hopeful conception of self-esteem difficulties. He points out that self-esteem is a current issue, not a past one. Low self-esteem results from guilt, and guilt is related to hurting others, breaking agreements with others, lying, and not living up to one's own value system. Such a perspective on self-esteem is hopeful because it rests upon factors over which one has some control. Childhood hurts are past, and cannot be undone. The notion that therapy can repair these early sufferings through catharsis, identifying cause-effect factors, and "working through" is simply a myth, or highly questionable faith, at best. Research does not support this hope. Realistic guilt as to the ordering of one's present life-style can be changed.

If guilt is a common ingredient of change efforts with both addiction and burnout, we have a serious dilemma. Low self-esteem appears almost inevitable, whether one tries to change a problematic pattern or not, as indicated above.

Is there a perspective we can use in burnout and addiction that will enable us to change our behavior without endangering our self-esteem? In the next part of the seminar we will consider ways of accomplishing this.

HOMEWORK

Three tasks are assigned as homework to be done prior to the second, and last, meeting together. Feedback will be expected.

(1) Attempt to change a troubling desire pattern, or to generate desire where it is lacking, and notice the inner chatter that is aroused within you. What are you telling yourself about your condition? Your fears? Your values?

(2) Read the short novel *A Christmas Carol* by Charles Dickens, or view a videotape of the story. What motivated Scrooge to change? How were his past, present, and future a part of this process?

(3) Have you ever experienced a profound change in your own life, or do you know someone well who experienced this? What seemed to be the context or circumstances for this change?

If the seminar is to be done in one full day of two and a half or three hours in the morning and the same time sequence in the afternoon, the homework could be eliminated. The leader could begin the afternoon session by having people reflect upon and then write down the types of inner chatter that they can remember being associated with their previous change efforts. Then the leader could ask them to reflect upon times in their lives of profound change and what seemed to be the content and circumstances of this change. This could be done in a 20-minute period, with 10 minutes devoted to each task of reflection. Since everyone is familiar with the tale of Scrooge, participants can later draw upon their memories of the story, and the group can reconstruct the appearances of Marley's ghost and the three visitations of ghosts from Christmas past, present, and future.

There are advantages to both formats. The break of a week allows for more personal investment by participants of time and effort in the three exercises. The single-day seminar, on the other hand, builds an intensity from the morning session that mounts into the afternoon program.

Chapter 12

RENEWAL OF BELIEF SYSTEMS

Seminar participants have been prepared for some new insights or solutions. Since the seminar leader has agreed that usual change efforts are inclined to fail, there is naturally an expectation for some new ideas. The intent of this second segment of the seminar is to convey the message that issues of addiction and burnout are not merely psychological matters. They have social and spiritual dimensions as well.

There are varied ways of talking about change that integrate psychological, social, and spiritual factors. I have a way of conceptualizing this process that I call the *renewal spiral*. The ingredients of the change process are drawn primarily from the self-help movement. Self-help groups have long incorporated the three dimensions of importance. My own conception includes ideas drawn from self-help spokesmen John Drakeford, Hobart Mowrer, and Keith Miller, as well as feminist spokeswoman Robin Norwood. The elements of the renewal spiral as I conceptualize it are shown in Figure 12.1.

Like the desire spiral, the renewal spiral can be viewed in two opposite ways. The process of renewal is a gradually expanding spiral that opens up awareness, interest, and appreciation to more and more aspects of life experience. At the same time, personal energy is not dispersed or dissipated, but rather focused more and more clearly upon the singular matter at hand.

Acceptance. The beginning of all self-help programs emphasizes strongly the attribute of acceptance. This includes acceptance by self, others, and God (or some power greater than oneself). This amounts to

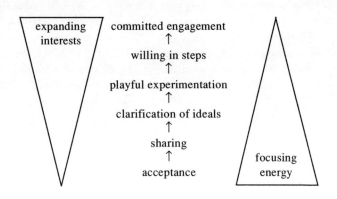

Figure 12.1 The Renewal System

letting oneself be fully aware of one's sense of conflict, shame, and powerlessness to change, and of being stuck and guilty (responsible).

Sharing. Acceptance is best facilitated by others who have been stuck in much the same way as you are now. It may therefore not be sufficient to share with your friends and relatives. This is why self-help groups of people who experienced similar problems become an important adjunct system of significant others. This is also why the value of a psychotherapist is in doubt, unless he or she has had the same problem and is willing to share this. Even then, psychotherapists tend to be advisers, authorities, and guides in a one-sided way (not sharing their own need for guidance). Here again, the self-help group is more real and potentially more useful in the long run. Self-help groups have traditionally been used for people with drug and alcohol addictions and mental illness, for parolees, and for those who want to lose weight or quit smoking. The use of such groups has been expanded successfully with a broad array of emotional problems (Mowrer, 1961) and spiritual floundering (Miller, 1987). The model of sharing often used is that of personal confession, which originated in religious communities centuries ago as a bonding action for group cohesion and trust.

Clarification of ideals. Whether speaking of heroes, heroines, archetypes, or images and symbols of religious or philosophical inspiration, people who are sensing their own powerlessness require some direction and hope that can be envisioned in a meaningful way. If a person is going to let go of some dominating desire or discover an empowering source of energy that will end burnout, he or she must somewhere transcend him- or herself. Since problems of addiction and burnout are also tied to social and family roles and forces, the transcending force needs to be powerful and greater than the societal forces in which one is already enmeshed. Self-willing is not sufficient, nor are the criticisms and complaints of worried significant others. Guilt and self-disgust call for hope, new direction, and a personal sense of affirmation. At this early stage of change a dramatic conversion of life direction may occur for a few; for most, however, there is a much slower process that begins with a reassessment of potentially hopeful or inspirational images. Is there some powerful and profound desire behind our numerous superficial and divergent desires that can be recognized?

Playful experimentation. The beginning experience of empowerment rests upon the realization that one can activate choices. Habit patterns of one's life-style may be challenged in an experimental way. One may do things one usually avoids, and not do things one usually does. One may recognize the multiple images and potentials of one's own identity and begin to play out roles ordinarily only fantasized. One may learn to say or do nothing in situations where one is commonly reactive. One will expose oneself to experiences and people that have been viewed as a threat. One will bring a halt to demands and criticisms and be willing to grieve for the loss of one's usual habit patterns. One will begin to act on guilt by ending guilt-inducing behavior and seeking ways to ask for forgiveness and make amends. Experimenting with life choices has the effect of unbalancing long-held beliefs and opening oneself up to new opportunities and potentials previously unknown.

Willing in steps. The new experiences resulting from playful experimentation enable one to see realistic ways of living out ideals. Ideals, especially opposing ones, are also clarified by the new life experiences and the continued sharing of these results with others. Reappraisals as to how to incorporate one's religion or philosophical perspective in one's daily life emerge naturally. One no longer sees one's self-esteem as so dependent upon another person or even upon the performance of a particular activity. There is a growing sense of personal integrity as being related to how one responds to the task at hand. One is content to limit desire spiral activity to levels of wishing and wanting. One may pursue activities with vitality and resolve, yet one's satisfaction is no longer wholly determined by the results. A willingness to risk replaces placid securities. Life becomes more adventurous, yet within a context of respecting existing responsibilities and loyalty to valued relationships with family and friends. These are the built-in guards against mistaking emerging passions for some new version of narcissistically directed "needs" that ignore others. The Gestalt "prayer" of Perls (1969) was both wrong and deceitful in this regard. One does not simply "do one's own thing" without regard to one's effect upon others.

Committed engagement. This is a matured understanding of one's place in the world of others. Spiritual direction is lived out through a world of valued relationships with others and the tasks of ordinary daily life. Self-indulgence is replaced by an allegiance to principles or, for some, a relationship in faith with a "divine presence." One feels addressed by the world and called upon to respond. One feels oneself to be a participant in a process, a context, a realm of unfolding mystery, a battle involving good and evil, spirit and death. One dwells in personal humility and humor, in relation to personal interests and wants. Experiences of emptiness and suffering are as much an expression of one's continued dialogue with life as pleasure and joy. One's tendencies to argue, justify, apologize, criticize, and react defensively are more and more diminished.

So much for a scheme of renewal. I have mentioned above the elements usually alluded to in the aforementioned programs for growth. Some emphasize certain aspects of the process and pay less attention to other elements that are underscored by other programs. Details for expanded exercises related to the growth stages are developed in the literature noted at the end of this chapter. These can be adapted, expanded upon, or ignored in accordance with the knowledge framework of the seminar leaders and in response to the interests of a particular audience.

The challenge for a seminar of this type is how to present the material in a fashion that can be understood by participants and related to their own experience. If one attempted to present a renewal process in the manner I have described it, the effort would be doomed to failure. It is too cognitive, and an audience would soon "tune out" because of content overload.

One needs to bear in mind a sound principle of effective teaching, that in any single class period one should present no more than a few new ideas. These need to be illustrated by examples, personal exercises, and discussions that include sharing of personal experiences. It is for this reason that follow-up self-help groups are recommended. In this particular session, seminar leaders need to convey a perspective of change that can be grasped and to imply the need for ongoing work by participants.

The leader must also be on guard, in such a presentation, to remain sensitive to the truths being grappled with, and not to distort the perspective to appear as THE SOLUTION. A very difficult process is being introduced, one that has variations, and participants will pick up on specific appealing ideas and ignore others. We are offering a path that can and will be traveled in numerous ways. If people are not to be disillusioned by "just another hopeful plan that doesn't work," they must somehow come to understand that this path needs to be individualized and adapted to varied belief systems.

Considering the framework described above, I will share one way of attempting to convey this orientation in this second seminar meeting. The homework assignments become the points of departure.

FEEDBACK ON INNER CHATTER
AND CHANGE EFFORTS

This second session is introduced with a brief, 5-minute review of the desire spiral and the difficulties encountered by change efforts. I include an example of a former participant who developed and used this simple motto:

If I am what I do, then if I don't, I'm not!

I expand the person's meaning of this motto. His sense of identity revolves around habit patterns—what he does to maintain comfort levels of "need" satisfactions. When he attempts to disrupt or stop one or more of these patterns of behavior, he experiences his sense of personal identity as somehow diminished. He has therefore made a very important discovery. Troubling desire-satisfaction patterns are not simply unwanted "foreign intrusions"; rather, they are owned and chosen behaviors that have become part of this person's valued personal identity. The elimination of such a pursuit can be experienced as a fearful or despairing personal loss of self.

Having set the stage, I invite participants to share with the total group the results of their first homework exercise. Using their inner chatter experiences generated from efforts to change a desire pattern (or, for many, even the consideration of such change), I help participants identify values and beliefs reflected by the inner chatter process. Examples shared reveal common fears and catastrophic expectations related to the possibility of change. This discussion can be handled much like the exercise feedback described in Chapter 2 that revealed common value positions related to problematic inner chatter. Valued security positions are validated as common, "normal," and usually reinforced by

family, friends, and various societal value ideas, such as through advertising and TV soap operas.

Seminar leaders may usefully share some of their own valued positions that were or are still problematic. The mood of this entire discussion should be light, so the use of humor and exaggerated dramatization
is important. Here the use of two seminar leaders can be helpful, as the
two can play off of each other and the participants for enhanced
spontaneity.

As participants share their beliefs, fears, and values, seminar leaders
actively engage them through questions that draw out more details. The
atmosphere tends to be that of public confessional borne up by strong
personal interest and acceptance. This segment of the meeting is not to
be rushed, for the more variance among fears and values is revealed,
the more learning there is for all. Many participants discover aspects of
their own life stances, usually ignored, in the confessions of others.
While participants are invited to expand upon their experiences, the
seminar leaders are also careful to limit the nature of the sharing. The
purpose is not to "therapize" anyone as to the historical traumas that
produced such beliefs, or to suggest alternate, "more realistic" beliefs,
but to clarify the beliefs and related value-security positions. If a
participant elaborates with historical explanations, these are dealt with
by clarifying the nature of the resulting belief and minimizing the value
of the source of the belief. The message is, "Past is past, what is
important is the conclusion you have arrived at and maintained."

Experientially, seminar participants are dealing with the first two
levels of the renewal spiral: *acceptance* and *sharing*. It is not uncom-
mon, during this discussion, for participants also to share resentments
and cynicism about motivational programs to which they have previously been exposed. A common denominator of group acceptance,
here, is the sense that "the harder you try, the worse it gets."

THE INSIGHT OF SCROOGE

Following a break, seminar leaders ask for feedback on the second
homework exercise. A diagram such as the following may provide a
guide for this discussion of Scrooge's experience:

```
Marley's ghost: fear and trembling
Ghost of Christmas Past: traumatic cause
Ghost of Christmas Present: unnerving mirror of self
Ghost of Christmas Future: fated consequences
```

Dickens's character of Scrooge is presented as evidencing behaviors that appear as both addiction and burnout. The addiction is miserliness. The burnout is a narrowed life-style that excludes human warmth and engagement. The story, *A Christmas Carol*, says little as to events preceding the Christmas Eve of the visitation by the three spirits. Perhaps Scrooge had been having episodes of mounting anxiety and sleepless nights—we simply don't know. But what happened that night to produce the profound change in Scrooge? The word *profound* is deliberately emphasized, as it will be tied again to the discussion of the third homework exercise of participants sharing memories of personal profound change.

The ensuing discussion of Scrooge's fictional experience is developed from the responses of participants. Several themes emerge from this story. There is the ongoing struggle of Scrooge with a sense of some unsettling unknown, and his efforts to minimize and rationalize away its importance. Then there are nostalgic early memories ringed with touches of self-pity and blame of others. Scrooge becomes increasingly disturbed as he sees himself, now, through the eyes of others and senses his personal desolation. What he usually perceives as security and a protective barrier against the world becomes more and more ominous. He is hurting others and himself as well. The price is too high, his losses too great. The unbearable confrontation, however, is with his own fate. His future is clear. His death displays the utter futility of his life-style. But his death also reveals something more: There is yet time. He need not be bound by who he was and who he is. He can surprise the world and lose nothing of real consequence.

The story of Scrooge speaks to us of isolated entrapment and hopeless despair. But it sings also of the power of the self-aware human spirit and its potential. It is clearly a message about profound change being rooted in personal value confrontation. It challenges popular assumptions of today's world: that suffering is to be avoided, and that painless, slick fixes are available for the asking. It implies, too, that a religious or spiritual dimension can be an extremely important ingredient of change. A resurrection of spirit can accompany the death of an outworn self. Scrooge exemplifies the change process found in religious conversion as well as in the road back from alcohol and drug addictions. Profound change is not merely a modification of behavior. Fundamental belief changes and life-style rearrangements are called forth.

This discussion of Scrooge provides an example with whom all are familiar. The tale illustrates a change so radical as to be inclusive of most people's struggles. Few would declare their personal problems as more extreme than those of Scrooge. Students are less threatened by envious reactions when an example is fiction rather than some personal testimonial. Even the religious-spiritual element of the story is one that can be easily related to most philosophical and religious frameworks. Finally, it is a story most people have known since childhood, a time of their own innocence in the face of a world of potent mysteries.

In relation to the concepts of the renewal spiral, students experience elements of *clarification of ideals* and *playful experimentation* as they recollect the struggles and changes in Scrooge. There is also a key idea introduced in this discussion: At the root of all of our desires may be a singular, more profound, desire. Gabriel Marcel differentiates on this point, between desire and hope (Padovano, 1966, p. 53). What we have referred to as a profound desire, Marcel would call hope. Desire has a specific, concrete object for its intended fulfillment. Hope, on the other hand, refers to an orientation toward life in general. We are moving closer to an understanding of the nature of change called for in relation to personal belief or value systems. For Scrooge, the affirmation of a primary and enlivening hope called for a profound disillusionment with what might be seen as secondary desires. Such is the nature of spiritual conversions.

FEEDBACK ON PROFOUND LIFE CHANGES

The third homework assignment requested participants to recollect times of profound change in their lives, and the circumstances thereof. I have found it most useful to begin this discussion with small group sharing. With groupings of four or five, there is adequate opportunity for all participants to share experiences. If some can recall no profound changes, they often may talk of such changes in others they have known. Group members begin to factor out and appreciate the variations as to what circumstances produce such changes. The foregoing discussion of Scrooge has established some important guidelines for participants' interests in one another's experience. During the course of these group exchanges, seminar leaders may wish to move among the groups, not only to gain some familiarity with ideas being discussed but also to assure that all participants have ample opportunity to share their personal recollections.

After ample time for the small group discussions has elapsed, the total group is reassembled and general feedback is invited. This feedback is directed toward the specific insights or conclusions that surfaced among the groups. These ideas typically take a variety of forms. Some people will assert that profound change was forced upon them, often involving intense pain and the repeated failure of efforts to deny specific realities of their life experience. Such pain may be physical, emotional, economic, or social. Pain may originate within themselves or in response to the effect their life-styles were having on others, usually family, friends, or fellow workers. The intensity of such pain would override those usual fears that impeded change. For others, pain did not seem forced upon them, but resulted from a failure and despair with values that had governed their lives. There would be guilt over the sense that one was living a lie or following some faulty illusion. A reexamination of values or life meaning was being called for. The unbalancing of formerly secure values resulted in some inner void or emptiness. Yet within this very dearth of values, within this chaotic confusion of motivations, they would find some inner strength. This is not unlike Paul Tillich's (1952) definition of courage: being grasped and affirmed by the power of Being in spite of having found oneself totally unacceptable (p. 164). This newfound strength would soon take the form of energy, which would pursue a new life direction.

Most people would not have conceptualized their own experiences of change in such elaborate, philosophical terms, but the group process itself invites those of a more philosophical bent to address the meanings of changes being described. Seminar leaders, who have already conceptualized some understanding of profound change, such as in the renewal spiral described above, use this general discussion to clarify and elaborate upon insights being shared. At this point the group is experientially dealing with the final two phases of the renewal process, *willing in steps* and *committed engagement*.

NEW DIRECTIONS

An interesting change has now occurred within the group. People who had sought out this seminar because of a sense of fear and helplessness are now talking from viewpoints that affirm potential strength and hope. They have discovered these perspectives within their own resources. Seminar leaders have become facilitators rather than preachers, motivators, or advisers. Notions of change are not focused upon slick, quick fixes or upon motivational slogans and self-hypnotic promises. Nor has change been mystified through reference to murky traumatic histories accessible only through the guidance of trained professionals. A linkage has been established between personal psychological struggles and useful truths potentially available through literary, philosophical, and religious sources.

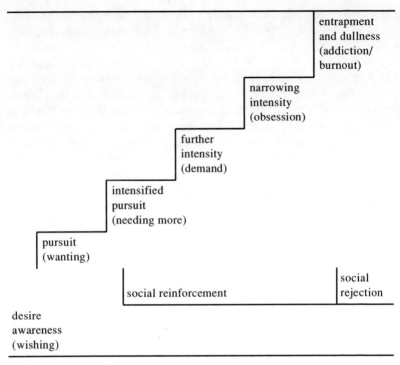

Figure 12.2 Summary of Desire Spiral

Yet in spite of this upbeat atmosphere, seminar leaders have a responsibility to return once again to the troubling matters that brought participants to the seminar in the first place. Leaders must ask, "Knowing of these important human ingredients of profound change, and (for some) having already undergone such change in the past, what can you do differently with your current difficulties of burnout or addiction?"

At this point it may be useful to summarize the desire spiral through the use of the diagram depicted in Figure 12.2. At the needing level social reinforcements are established, alghough these may turn to rejections at the level of addiction. The point may be made that passion can be playful at the levels of wishing and wanting. Beyond this, desires tend toward idolization, that is, they are linked up with some personal definition of happiness or security. Desire intensifies as it works its way up the spiral. The greater the intensity, the greater the pain of loss called for in the act of letting go of the desire. Some redefinition of happiness or security is called for. This seems eventually to require radical disillusionment. A profound and primary hope may await, but this is as yet unknown. Such a hope may place all subsequent desires in a new light. There is a grieving process called for, since one will lose a valued piece of one's own identity in the change process. The need for others is called for by this grief process. The spiritual search has this interpersonal dimension.

At this point self-help alternatives need to be discussed. Robin Norwood (1985, chap. 10) describes the use of self-help groups that include a spiritual dimension but are not associated with any particular religious or philosophical faith. Keith Miller (1987) and Hobart Mowrer (1961) describe the formation and use of self-help groups within religious settings. There is no reason a self-help process cannot be initiated within groups of family members or among friends, although these have the added risk of other agendas too often related to stereotyped roles and selfish needs for security. Seminar leaders may offer to provide initial leadership (ten sessions) for a self-help group made up of those participants so inclined. Such groups could be focused upon generic issues of burnout and addiction or (depending on the group interest) upon a specific problem area, such as workaholism. There will be some participants who would prefer to associate with some existing self-help program, such as Alcoholics Anonymous or Recovery, Inc.

Evaluation forms are provided to all participants, and these should include a question regarding some plan for action. If members need more information on groups, or if they want to sign up for self-help groups facilitated by the seminar leaders, provision is made on the form for these requests.

Chapter 13

SELF-HELP PROGRAMS

As indicated in Chapter 12, those seminar participants who wish to join a self-help group initiated by the seminar leaders and involving their participants may want a generic focus upon burnout and addiction issues in keeping with the seminar focus. Others may prefer a specific problem-oriented group, such as a group for workaholics or alcoholics. I will begin this discussion with a plan for the generic self-help group, as this is the most popular.

Since each seminar group is unique in makeup, the nature of the follow-up group is best left up to the gradually emerging interests of the specific group. For this reason, readings are assigned each time in the first three sessions, using either books or printouts on the ideas of Hobart Mowrer, Keith Miller, and Robin Norwood. These include Alcoholics Anonymous's 12-step program as redesigned for a broad spectrum of addiction issues, such as substance abuse, sex-related problems, emotional problems, eating disorders, and codependency. Since the group is expected to function without leaders after the tenth meeting, it is especially important that the members build their own rules and expectations.

Seminar facilitators need to be well acquainted with the perspectives in all readings assigned so as to be able to bring these to the group as experiences within the group and as homework assignments. Mowrer (1961), for instance, sets forth three principles: honesty, taking responsibility, and emotional involvement. These activities can be demonstrated and worked with in any or all meetings. Norwood (1985), on the other hand, sets forth specific tasks for homework experimentation and subsequent feedback to the group.

Using the renewal spiral stages of change, I have incorporated the following group exercises and format that can be adopted with variations during the first ten sessions.

ACCEPTANCE AND SHARING

The first two phases are intertwined. Miller (1987), like Mowrer (1961), emphasizes the primary value of sharing as much preferable to advice-giving tendencies of group members. According to Miller, sharing requires self-honesty, including being able to verbalize fears of exposure of feelings. Sharing is not only in the form of problems with which one is struggling, but also in the form of experiences related to the problems set forth by others. Group members take turns being helper and helpee. Acceptance is underscored as all members set forth personal problems of both past and present related to the focus of the group. Failures and the state of "stuckness" are a common bond. Miller emphasizes that the early phase of such group life consists of an "unraveling and opening up." This is much like Mowrer's principle of emotional engagement, wherein group members are expected not only to share feelings of frustration and grief about themselves, but to demonstrate a caring interest in response to the problems of others.

Since readings are assigned, it is important that the group does not focus upon an intellectual discussion of responses to readings. A more useful beginning for each session is that described by Miller. Participants take turns in the leadership role, and each meeting begins with the leader inquiring who has a personal issue they would like to bring up. If there are no volunteers, the leader shares an issue of his or her own. Ideas from the readings are incorporated in the same way as personal experiences, that is, in relation to a particular personal issue that is under discussion. Miller's rule is listen, take what is helpful in solutions posed by the experiences of others, and don't criticize. Confrontation in relation to apparent avoidance or denial is not done unless specifically requested by the party concerned.

CLARIFICATION OF IDEALS

Clarification of ideals is a way of helping people take responsibility for their personal issues. Exercises that may be useful as homework assignments are those described for the graduate course on practice wisdom: heroes, heroines, and models; archetype exploration; guilt inventory; exploring ideas about G___; and attitudes about organized religion.

Mowrer clarifies how realistic guilt is related to troubling emotions and requires some decision for change and a commitment to the group in relation to change effort. Miller, on the other hand, uses the term *sin* and defines this as a sense of separateness, a feeling of being unworthy and unacceptable. The addict, then, seeks to handle this underlying pain through control efforts. He or she seeks to establish some sense of involvement, emotional dependency from outside him- or herself. The demand is for more and more satisfaction, progressing toward a state of personal grandiosity in terms of expectations. Judgment is increasingly impaired, with denial being a chief characteristic. Such self-deception and manipulation form another way of talking about realistic guilt. Mowrer sets forth realistic ideals in his principles of honesty, responsibility, and emotional involvement. These can be related to and embellished from a variety of religious or philosophical orientations. For those lacking such orientations, these principles can usually be integrated with models or archetype images valued.

Norwood (1985) agrees that the basic problem is one of control. She emphasizes the importance of spirituality in relation to letting go of habitual control efforts. If one is in an addictive relationship, one needs a new source of relationship affirmation to replace it. This new source must be of a spiritual nature, based in trust and inspiration, or one will simply set up a new version of an addictive relationship with someone else. Self-will battles of inner conflict will diminish only when one discovers a nurturing spiritual grounding. Norwood even suggests an exercise of using affirming images related to a spiritual orientation to replace the inner chatter usually generated by the problem in question.

Playful experimentation and *willing in steps* are a continuum of behavioral efforts. One activates choices and initiates new behaviors as a means of rediscovering one's personal power and possibilities. Later behavioral and attitudinal changes are integrated with a growing sense of one's personal integrity and life-style direction.

Changes in habit patterns by means of alternate behaviors or shifted thinking result in an unbalancing of mind-sets. When one begins to experience confusion, uncertainty, or new ways of being, there is an opening up of awareness to new inputs. Suffering, joy, new possibilities, and unfinished business may arise to consciousness. Some tasks for the group are designed to unbalance mind-sets; others help people address resulting shifts in awareness; still others enable members to begin tracking new possibilities. Here is a list of potential tasks.

UNBALANCING TASKS

- Doing/not doing: Do something you usually avoid, but that you think may be good for you. Or stop doing something you usually do but that you believe you would be better off without.
- Role switching: Our roles for relating to others vary with situations and expectations. Select one of your roles (parent, friend, adult/child, employee, consumer) and act it in a situation wherein you usually use a different role.
- Expand your personal environment by exposing yourself to new people or experiences, and be aware of the effect this has upon you.

Norwood (1985) suggests the following for the same unbalancing purpose:

- Permit yourself to grieve. A loss need not be that of a person, it may just as well be a valued activity.
- Let go of making demands of others. This will not only relieve guilt directly, but open up new options in relationships.
- Let yourself say or do nothing when you usually act.
- Say no when you are tempted to qualify or hedge.
- Say yes when you typically express uncertainty.

HEIGHTENING AWARENESS

- Permit yourself quiet times of reflection or meditation so that you are able to attend to arising possibilities, unfinished business, or pain of any sort that is there. How are you being addressed by life? What needs doing? Be gentle with your self-expectations and criticisms.
- Embrace emptiness (an exercise suggested by Norwood). Emptiness will commonly occur when you shift habitual patterns, especially when they are part of addictive behavior.
- Keep a journal (another recommendation made by Norwood). Journaling is one of the direct routes to fostering a sense of personal integrity and direction. Norwood suggests listing in your journal what you feel good about or what makes you uncomfortable or unhappy. Journaling provides an opportunity for you to explore painful memories that reoccur. It also provides an alternative to depending too much upon the opinions of others.

TRACKING NEW POSSIBILITIES

- Reappraise your image ideals in relation to those activities and attitudes that are compatible with such beliefs. Are you behaving in line with your values?
- Prioritize your changes. Which ones are possible now? Which ones need to be delayed, and for how long?
- Cultivate a clarity as to what needs doing in your life (suggested by Norwood). Pursue your emerging interests. Try one new activity each week.
- Tolerate disapproval without argument, apology, or justification (another of Norwood's recommendations).

Any tasks attempted become food for group discussion, providing inspiration and excitement for others who have been tenuous and shy about initiating change. All tasks are potential avenues for taking responsibility in one's life, especially when one commits oneself in the group to such an effort. Excuses for not having performed such planned tasks are often challenged by the group.

The final phase of the renewal spiral, *committed engagement*, is not addressed through tasks. Committed engagement is an emerging awareness of how one conducts one's life based upon integrity, vitality, and responsiveness to a growing sense of destiny.

Miller (1987) wisely underscores typical group reactions that impede change. It is most difficult for people to realize how avoidance, denial, and self-centeredness continue to plague their good intentions. In church groups, especially, people may complain about too much emphasis on negative matters. They may prefer to shift the focus to inspirational discussions or moving more toward a prayer group. People must be allowed to leave the self-help group without condemnation if they conclude that such self-exploration is not for them.

Miller also points out that the intimacy of such groups is difficult to maintain. Discussions are shifted by group members from the personal to the impersonal, from the concrete to the abstract, from action to theory. These efforts represent avoidance of the personal need to be addressed by the group as a whole. The question of what it is that group members want or don't want to happen in the group must be addressed.

Another difficulty cited by Miller is people's impatience with the sharing process itself. This takes the form of group members' giving advice and criticizing others for failure or unwillingness to risk. Miller points out that the group needs to affirm, at such times, the value of honesty in sharing one's own experience as preferable to judgmental statements about others.

If a group is organized around a specific problem, such as alcoholism, workaholism, or eating or smoking addictions, it is most useful to follow the 12-step program. This program, originated by Alcoholics Anonymous, has been generalized for application to any addictions group. Two sources for such a guide are Miller's book and the Compcare publication *The Twelve Steps for Everyone* (Grateful Members, 1975).

Self-help groups differ from support groups found in mental health centers in the avoidance of professional leadership. If seminar leaders facilitate the organization of a self-help group for ten sessions, it is quite important that they consistently sidestep bids by group members for their professional opinions. Readings should be the resources for potential group direction. Leadership is shared by all group members, taking turns. Seminar leaders simply facilitate the organizational process and help the group to discover its personal focus and direction. After ten sessions the seminar facilitators choose whether they wish to leave the group or remain as nonpaid members.

APPENDIX:
HINTS FOR TEACHERS

COURSE STRUCTURE

Faculty have too often applied their exaggerated fears about client fragility to students in the classroom. Personal awareness through class exercises has been acceptable as a means of illustrating specific learning concepts, such as clear versus dysfunctional communication, core conditions (warmth, genuineness, and empathy), games illustrating power tactics, role plays on interviewing strategies, and experiencing group process. But to have students address their personal problems or to sort through the elements of their own identities, or to observe and share their here-and-now personal process while undergoing stress, has been historically relegated to the realm of their personal psychotherapy.

Field teachers, on the other hand, have occasionally been more daring. Students' personal struggles with "use of self," with transference and countertransference, with the identification of their own blind spots and personal vulnerability in relation to reactiveness to clients are considered important facets of experiential learning. These are observed and discussed in several contexts: the supervisor-student relationship, taped interviews, use of one-way mirror observation of interviews, cotherapist roles with students and supervisors or other staff, and self-awareness therapy groups that include several students and one or more field supervisors.

A common complaint of students resulting from this split between class and field is that classroom learning is too conceptual and lacking in personal relevance. Lectures and class discussions seem too far removed from the specific challenges encountered with clients in the field setting. Classroom teachers are commonly accused of being out of touch with direct practice.

A related dilemma, seldom voiced directly by students, is that those students undergoing private psychotherapy are often confused as to how to relate their personal therapeutic experiences with what they are learning in their professional education and field experiences. Since students seek out psychotherapists for their problems on their own, the nature of the therapy they experience may be quite different from, and even oppositional to, what they are expected to do in their practice with clients in field settings.

COURSE DESCRIPTION

Prior to signing up for my course on personal growth, students are alerted to the nature of the self-awareness component of the course by the brief description set forth in the curriculum offerings. This permits students who feel no need for such personal exploration, or who fear such a venture, to bypass the course. Since the course is offered at different times during their two years of study, students may feel more ready for or in need of such an effort at different times. The course is offered for all social work students regardless of their specialty area of study. Potential administrators or planners benefit from such personal awareness efforts as much as do students involved in direct practice with clients.

The course begins with a presentation of the elements of practice wisdom, as described in this volume's Introduction: theory, religion/philosophy, and personal subjective experience. These are related to learning how one uses oneself in relation to practice situations. Students usually share their own experiences as to when these three elements of human understanding have seemed integrated for them and when they have not. It is reassuring to students to realize that the very process of learning new knowledge and being exposed to new experiences in the field naturally produces confusion, inconsistencies, and awkward reactions. In order to learn and move toward new points of integration, one must be willing to allow the disintegration of former conclusions, beliefs, and habitual uses of self in helping roles. The resulting anxiety that tends to accompany this "normalizing reassurance" is quickly channeled into understanding the format of the course (see Figure A.1).

Dyad and journal sharing. The results of personal awareness exercises are shared by students in two ways. In the first class, each student

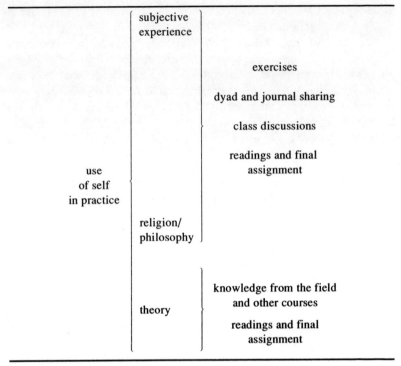

Figure A.1 Course Format

selects a partner with whom to share weekly exercise results throughout the course (10 or 15 weeks, depending on quarter or semester system). Students plan time outside of class for these dyad discussions. This expectation commonly arouses anxiety, which is usually relieved by the first or second experience in sharing. The experience of such sharing is often viewed as an appreciation of what a client might experience as he or she encounters the first interview with a helping professional. As the course progresses, anxieties over sharing are rekindled as students anticipate judgment, alarm, and differences in relation to experiences and attitudes to be shared. Their courage and efforts to understand result in both relief and an affirming appreciation of each other.

Each student maintains a weekly journal that is shared with the instructor two or three times during the course (about every four weeks). Journals include four parts: responses to exercises, responses to dyad sharing, responses to class discussion and lectures, and responses to readings. Journaling provides a threefold value. First, this process informs the instructor as to how all students are responding to the course, whether they have been verbal participants in the class or not. Second, the process gives the instructor an opportunity to reassure and challenge students in relation to their anxieties and conclusions. Third, the process helps students to become familiar with a technique for self-appraisal, tracking of their subjective experience, and creative reflection that can become a most useful self-therapeutic and integrative tool beyond the limits of the course itself. Practice wisdom will call for an ongoing process of this nature in the years ahead.

Class discussions. The teacher supplements awareness experiences with ideas presented through short lectures, role plays, and the use of tapes. These ideas provide a context for provoking, expanding, challenging, and reflecting upon the meanings students bring to the class from exercises and readings. The ideas are a combination of psychological, social, and spiritual perspectives. They are varied so as to allow students from differing theoretical, religious, or philosophical viewpoints to relate to conceptual ideas. The subsequent discussions within the class are dealt with by the teacher so as to affirm different beliefs. Cultural and sex-role differences are highlighted as well. The classroom becomes a forum for pluralistic searches for truth. It is important for the teacher to model a willingness to share personal opinions and prejudices while accepting, understanding, and affirming viewpoints quite different from his or her own.

Readings and final assignment. A bibliography is presented to students in the first class, with a brief commentary on each potential reading. The bibliography I use is included as the References to this volume, but each teacher naturally will want to construct a list of readings with which he or she is familiar. My own list is somewhat slanted toward material usually associated with existential and humanistic psychology. I find this literature especially useful because of its emphasis upon philosophical ideas in addition to perspectives on how one uses oneself personally in the practice arena. Students are encouraged to select readings that are most in keeping with their present interests and pursuit of knowledge. They may add selections of personal appeal that are not in the bibliography, although these are to be discussed in advance with the instructor, because of the nature of the final assignment.

The final assignment represents another step in the student's effort at personal integration. I usually request a statement of philosophical perspective, an integration of this with practice, and a critique of the special values and shortcomings of this combined effort. A teacher may further request that students apply research substantiation and case examples to illustrate their practice perspectives.

Knowledge from the field and other courses. The theme of practice wisdom is integration. Students are encouraged to bring into class reactions to their experiences, struggles, and observations from work in the field. What actually happens with their clients is often a powerful test of what they are learning about use of self in this course. As they sharpen personal ethical and philosophical issues for themselves, they are able to question some of the attitudes and practices toward clients that are apparent among agency staff. Students discover not only that they are changing certain aspects of their own roles with clients, but that they are perceiving clients in new ways. As they become less preoccupied with categorization of people, with fears of client fragility, and with their own exaggerated self-expectations as "rescuers," they discover enhanced client responsiveness to their own relaxed spontaneity.

Since the way of practice wisdom calls for integration of theory with both religious/philosophical views and subjective experience, it becomes important for students to discuss in class varied theoretical perspectives. These stem from other courses, field teachers, and their readings. It is true that each psychological or social theory is based upon a set of specific philosophical assumptions, yet it is also possible to utilize specific concepts and treatment methods from various theories by framing them within one's personal philosophical perspective. An obvious example of this has been how Freudian psychology was easily adapted in schools of pastoral psychology despite Freud's obvious hostility toward religion. Thus pastoral counselors had no trouble making the id a bed partner with the Holy Spirit!

Students come to this course expecting some unbalancing of their secured ideas. They hope to be challenged. While readings and class discussions of ideas are aimed at provocation and expansion of thinking, the most powerful pressure comes from the exercises and from the dyadic discussions of them. Here students confront unknowns within themselves and between themselves and their partners. An arena is created for peer learning. The purpose and format of the course must be clear in order for students to proceed with a certain sense of safety and trust.

DISCUSSING RELIGION

Chapter 8 approaches a delicate area for many teachers. Graduate programs, except when taught in religious institutions, have carefully avoided in-depth discussions of religion. Included in Chapter 8 is a list of eight statements useful for stimulating thought and discussion. It should be obvious from this set of statements that I intend to focus the discussion around religious ideas, and especially those related to the Judeo-Christian tradition. I will share the kinds of ideas that I have found personally useful, knowing that these also reflect some of my own preferences and bias. A teacher need not be well grounded in religion and philosophy to handle such a class discussion; however, I do believe it is useful for students to have some sense of what the teacher believes. Even more important, perhaps, is how the teacher demonstrates intelligent tolerance for viewpoints with which he or she might disagree. If a teacher knows little about varied religions, there is a useful alternative to handling this discussion. First, a class session can be held in which students share their personal attitudes on institutional religion. This can be followed in the next class by a panel of social workers from the community representing intelligent and committed stances on Catholic, Protestant, and Jewish faiths, as well as a nonreligious professional. The teacher could begin the panel discussion by summarizing the attitudes and criticisms of students from the previous class. The panel would then respond, and a lively student and panel interchange would be in the making.

I usually begin this class by commenting that we have touched on ideas not only from existential philosophy, but from Buddhism, Hinduism, and Native American religions. On the other hand, the Judeo-Christian religions are the ones understood by most of our clients and the ones with which we are most familiar by family tradition. By putting this discussion in the context of other religions and philosophical ideas already discussed, one is free as a teacher personally to affirm Judeo-Christian ideas in the classroom if one wishes to do so.

A teacher need not be defensive in response to students' criticisms of religion. One may even share some of one's personal frustrations with the apparent misuses and abuses of religion. I have found it useful to point out that the deceptive hideouts people sometimes seem to find in religion are found also in the more popular philosophies and psychologies of the day. Therapies, for example, have been too often "guru-ized"—promising enlightened maturity through reason, or a "flowering

actualization" of joy and liberation, or the promise of a "quick fix" for
annoying symptoms or family members interrupting one's otherwise
comfortable life-style (Krill, 1986).

DISCUSSING SOCIAL ACTION

A notable lack in my course presentation has been the linkage of
experiences in class with issues of social change, social action, community planning, or administration. This is so partly because of my personal limits of scope, and partly because the practice wisdom quest
seems to call for beginning with oneself and one's more intimate
relationships. When students focus upon broad political issues, social
problems, and elaborate planning before having confronted themselves
as persons, there is a strong tendency for them to avoid the personal
search altogether, and the eventual result tends toward cynicism or
authoritarianism rather than practice wisdom. There is a relevant quote
on this matter by Yasutani-roshi, a modern Zen master:

> There are many people who spend all their time giving aid to the needy
> and joining movements for the betterment of society. To be sure, this ought
> not to be discounted. But their root anxiety, growing out of their false view
> of themselves and the universe, goes unrelieved, gnawing at their hearts
> and robbing them of a rich, joyous life. Those who sponsor and engage in
> such social betterment activities look upon themselves, consciously or
> unconsciously, as morally superior and never bother to purge their minds
> of greed, anger, and delusive thinking. But the time comes when, having
> grown exhausted from all their restless activity, they can no longer conceal
> from themselves their basic anxieties about life and death. Then they
> seriously begin to question why life hasn't more meaning and zest. Now
> for the first time they wonder whether instead of trying to save others they
> ought not to save themselves first. (Kapleau, 1966, p. 140)

If, on the other hand, one wishes to focus upon social action and
political issues, two books I have found related to the philosophy
presented herein are *Radical Man*, by Charles Hampton-Turner, and *The
Pornography of Power*, by Lionel Rubinoff. I also address some of these
issues in "The Absurd Social Activist," in *Existential Social Work.*
(Krill, 1978, chap. 11).

STAFF DEVELOPMENT PROGRAMS

Professional agencies are always seeking staff development programs. This is an opportunity for faculty to become more directly
involved with field agencies. A common frustration of staffs is the
burnout and floundering over practice demands. The material in this
book relating to understanding and developing practice wisdom, as well
as the content on burnout and addiction, provides a lucrative source for
staff development programs. Such teaching might be focused in varied
ways, depending on the needs of an agency. For some there will be
interest in the personal awareness emphasis of the practice wisdom
content. For others there may be a more pragmatic interest in an eclectic
model, such as ideas similar to those discussed in Chapter 6. There will
also be occasions when the problems of burnout and addiction among
staff members (or their target population of treatment) would be respon-
sive to the content of Chapters 11, 12, and 13.

REFERENCES

Anderson, C. (1970). Assumption centered psychotherapy. In R. Jurjervich (Ed.), *Direct psychotherapy: 28 American originals.* Miami: University of Miami.

Assagioli, R. (1965). *Psychosynthesis: A manual of principles and techniques.* New York: Hobbs, Dorman.

Becker, E. (1973). *The denial of death.* New York: Free Press.

Bloom, A. (1987). *The closing of the American mind.* New York: Simon & Schuster.

Borowitz, E. B. (1966). *A layman's introduction to religious existentialism.* New York: Delta.

Castaneda, C. (1972). *Journey to Ixtlan.* New York: Simon & Schuster.

Corsini, R., Standal, J., & Stanelly, W. (1959). *Critical incidents in psychotherapy.* Englewood Cliffs, NJ: Prentice-Hall.

Dhopeshwarkar, A. D. (1967). *J. Krishnamurti and awareness in action.* Bombay: Popular Prakashan. (Distributed by Humanities Press, New York)

Ellis, A. (1974). *Humanistic psychotherapy: The rational-emotive approach.* New York: McGraw-Hill.

Fagan, J., & Shepard, I. L. (Eds.). (1970). *Gestalt therapy now.* Palo Alto, CA: Science & Behavior.

Farrelly, F. (1974). *Provocative therapy.* Madison, WI: Family, Social, Psychotherapy Service.

Frankl, V. (1965). *The doctor and the soul: From psychotherapy to logotherapy.* New York: Knopf.

Friedman, M. S. (1960). *Martin Buber: The life of dialogue.* New York: Harper & Row.

Grateful Members. (1975). *The twelve steps for everyone . . . who really wants them.* Minneapolis: Compcare.

Jung, C. G. (1958). *Psyche and symbol.* Garden City, NY: Doubleday.

Kapleau, P. (1966). *The three pillars of Zen.* New York: Harper & Row.

Kempler, W. (1973). *Principles of Gestalt family therapy.* Costa Mesa, CA: Kempler Institute.

Krill, D. F. (1978). *Existential social work.* New York: Free Press.

Krill, D. F. (1986). *The beat worker: Humanizing social work practice and psychotherapy.* Lanham, MD: University Press of America.

Krishnamurti, J. (1968). *Talks and other dialogues.* New York: Avon.

Krishnamurti, J. (1971). *The flight of the eagle.* New York: Harper & Row.

Lewis, C. S. (1947). *The abolition of man.* New York: Macmillan.

Maslow, A. H. (1962). *Toward a psychology of being.* Princeton, NJ: Van Nostrand.

Miller, K. (1987). *Sin: Overcoming the ultimate deadly addiction.* San Francisco: Harper & Row.

Mowrer, O. H. (1961). *The crisis of psychiatry and religion.* Princeton, NJ: Van Nostrand.

Neil, J. R., & Kriskern, D. P. (1982). *From psyche to system: The evolving therapy of Carl Whittaker.* New York: Guilford.

Nichols, M. (1984). *Family therapy concepts and methods.* New York: Gardner.

Norwood, R. (1985). *Women who love too much.* New York: Pocket Books.

Offman, W. (1976). *Affirmation and reality, fundamentals of humanistic existential therapy and counseling.* Los Angeles: Western Psychological Services.

Padovano, A. T. (1966). *The estranged god: Modern man's search for belief.* New York: Sheed & Ward.

Peck, S. (1987). *The different drum: Community making and peace.* New York: Simon & Schuster.

Perls, F. S. (1969). *Gestalt therapy verbatim.* Lafayette, CA: Real People.

Reinhardt, K. F. (1960). *The existential revolt.* New York: Frederick Unger.

Reynolds, D. K. (1984). *Playing ball on running water.* New York: Quill.

Schaer, H. (1950). *Religion and the cure of souls in Jung's psychology.* New York: Pantheon.

Strean, H. F. (1979). *Psychoanalytic theory and social work practice.* New York: Free Press.

Streller, W. (1960). *Jean-Paul Sartre: To freedom condemned.* New York: Philosophical Library.

Tillich, P. (1952). *The courage to be.* New Haven, CT: Yale University Press.

Yalom, I. D. (1980). *Existential psychotherapy.* New York: Basic Books.

ABOUT THE AUTHOR

Donald F. Krill has taught at the University of Denver, Graduate School of Social Work, since 1967. His specialty field is direct practice with families and individuals, emphasizing an existential-interpersonal model of client understanding. He has also supervised students in field placements, and has had his own private practice for 28 years. At the university, he planned, developed, and administered the Family Therapy Training Center for postgraduate training of helping professionals. Prior to teaching, he served as a clinical social worker with the University of Colorado Medical Center for 8 years. He is internationally known for his writings on existential social work. In addition to articles, he has published two books, *Existential Social Work* (Free Press, 1978) and *The Beat Worker* (University Press of America, 1986). His current projects include consultation with Pueblo Indian tribes on the use of sequential network therapy (resource building for Indian families that have problems with alcoholism) and the development of volunteer lay-couple counselors for marital and family ministries with the poor. He is currently developing a book on the spiritual dimensions of social work practice.